We live in a decadent age. Young people no longer respect their parents. They inhabit taverns and have no self-control.

Inscription translated
from an Egyptian tomb,
written more than 6,000 years ago

Be calm, stoical, impassive. Do not show anger. Smile at misfortune. If you sprain your ankle, laugh.

Tiger Tinaka's advice to
secret agent 007, James Bond,
You Only Live Twice

In the beginning he used to shake his head and wonder how it could be that the children understood everything that I said and almost nothing that he said; and then he laughed at me when I told him that neither of us could teach the children anything, but that they could teach us.

Dostoyevsky, *The Idiot*

Dynamite Counselors Don't Explode!

A Complete Survival Course
For Child-Care Workers & Camp Counselors

by

Michael Pastore

Zorba Press
Lake Alexander
Dayville, Connecticut

Zorba Press gives generous discounts to libraries and non-profit organizations, and for large orders. Write to:

Special Sales Coordinator
Zorba Press
P.O. Box 666
Dayville, CT 06241
USA

Printed in the United States of America.
First Edition: April 1993

10 9 8 7 6 5 4 3 2 1

Library of Congress Catalog Card Number: 92-82030
ISBN: 0-927379-64-3
ZP 50

ZORBA PRESS ON LAKE ALEXANDER
DAYVILLE, CONNECTICUT

Contents

Foreword by Arthur Sharenow, CCD   vii

I MISTAKES GROWN-UPS ALWAYS MAKE WITH KIDS

1. How To Be The Worst Counselor On Earth 3
2. Are You A Robot Counselor? A Self-Evaluation Test 6
3. You're Ugly And Your Mother Dresses You Funny:
   More Mistakes Most Grown-ups Make 10

II HOW TO UNDERSTAND CHILDREN and
HOW TO GIVE CHILDREN WHAT THEY NEED

4. The Martian From Jupiter: Glimpses Of The
   Nature of The Child 19
5. How To Give Children What They Need:
   The 10 Basic Principles of Child Maintenance 22
6. Inside The Child: How To Use Empathy
   To Understand Children's Feelings And Needs 24
• Answers To Counseling Test & Martian From Jupiter 26

III WHAT GREAT COUNSELORS DO

7. What's It Really Like? One Day
   In The Life Of A Camp Counselor 28
8. The Secrets Of Working With Children 33

IV HOW TO PLAY and HAVE FUN WITH THE KIDS

9. Breaking The Ice: How To Play
   16 Getting Acquainted Games 38
10. Ready Set GO! How To Play Active Outdoor Games 43

V   BASIC COUNSELING SKILLS

11. How To Manage The First Moments & First Day   54
12. When and How To Say "No!" To Children   60
13. How To Get The Kids To Sleep At Bedtime   63

VI THE COUNSELOR AS LEADER

14. How To Plan A Game and Teach Activities   68
15. How To Create Togetherness
    With Your Group Of Children   73
16. How To Lead Open Meetings   76

VII CAMPING OUTDOORS WITH CHILDREN

17. Planning The Overnight Camping Trip   80
18. Basic Outdoor Living Skills   86

VIII COUNSELING TIPS

19. 50 Counseling Tips From Aardvarks To Zippers   94
20. Summer Camp Jobs: How To Find Them,
    How To Get Them, & How To Keep Them   103

APPENDIXES & SERENDIPITY

Appendix A. Useful Forms for Planning Hikes & Camping Trips   109
Appendix B. The Zorba Press Registered Reader Program   115

About the Author   116
Great Books from Zorba Press   117
Order Form for Zorba Press Books   118

Foreword By Arthur Sharenow, CCD

The very essence of a positive camp experience lies in the relationships which develop between campers and their counselors.

Each generation of Camp Directors rediscover this essential truth. Michael Pastore is a relative newcomer to the camping field, having directed a camp for only the past three summers. We are fortunate that Mr. Pastore, whose first professional field is as a much published author, has elected to share both of his skills with his camping brethren.

I, on the other hand, am an unpublished author but a very experienced Camp Director, having devoted the past thirty-three years to running the very best summer camp I can. I commend this book to you, whatever your experience. It has given me some new insights and ideas; suggested some valuable ways to articulate concepts to counselors; and provided me with the joy of a few hours of entertaining reading on my very favorite subject.

Michael Pastore has written what he believes to be a counselor manual. He writes amusingly and clearly, and his prose style likely will strike a respondent chord in the minds of young counselors. However, I believe he has written something more important than a counselor manual. He has written a primer for Camp Directors to use in working with their counselor staffs. Large sections of this book can be adapted for use during counselor orientation period, while other sections can be doled out to hungry counselors looking for emotional nourishment and support. *This book should be read by Camp Directors and other adult youth care workers*. It is our task to read, to think, to use and to adapt from this colorful text.

The first chapter in Part One, *Mistakes Grownups Always Make With Kids* (see pages 3 to 5), provides a litany of counselor sins. The Camp Director's first reaction might be: "Not in my camp. My counselors would never do those things." Just set your young counselors loose on a group of children without guidance and supervision and then watch as all of these sins occur. Even with good supervision and guidance some of them may occur. Using this list of mistakes with your staff, using them as examples of things that must not occur, will substantially reduce the risk.

The Camp Director might also want to lift intact the three exercises titled *The King of the Kreeps*. The characters are colorful and readily recognizable. Counselors may not want to see themselves in these caricatures, but they will readily recognize their friends. Neatly tucked away in this chapter is a pearl.

"Your words to children are either weapons or gifts. If you hurt a child's feelings he will never forget it, he will never forgive you, and he will never respect you."

The essential truth of this statement is crystal clear, and Mr. Pastore's hyperbole is entirely forgivable.

Chapters 7 and 8 have so many great quotes. A Camp Director could rearrange these ideas in any order that he or she chooses, and make them the opening night talk to new counselors. The one I like best is found on page 28. "The counselors who get the most from camp are the counselors who get their happiness from giving: giving of themselves, sharing, making other persons happy, helping children to learn and grow."

Chapter 9 contains many fine ice breakers, some of which are at least as applicable for use the first night of Staff Orientation as they might be for use by counselors with their campers on the first day of the camp season. Chapter 10 is a good reference library for counselors to use on all of those occasions where something non-traditional and innovative will serve to give the camp and campers a boost. I particularly liked the game # 15, *Mythology Tag*. Any game that has characters named Wizard, Dragon,

Mermaid, Serpent and Unicorn has a head start in appeal to younger campers.

Chapter 11 starts with another of the author's profound truths.

"The first moment you meet the child is the most important moment of the entire summer ... Children will trust and respect any grownup who takes the time to listen."

Pastore makes his arguments with a sharp point and then colors them with a broad brush. The very first day of camp is indeed the time to set the pattern of trust and friendship and caring that will last a season and hopefully a lifetime.

Chapter 12, *When and How To Say No to Children,* contains Michael's short list of "The Three Noes". These may be viewed as his camp counselor equivalent of the Ten Commandments. Chapter 13, *How to Get The Kids to Sleep at Bedtime,* should be mandatory reading. Getting campers to bed at night has been the single activity which has caused more irrational and ineffective counseloring than any other I have observed through the years. The concept of a "timed approach" to bedtime might well ameliorate the most urgent counselor instinct—to end the day with his or her campers and to begin private "adult" social time.

Most of the other chapters are straightforward HOW-TO guides to activities and leadership. They will be particularly valuable for you to share with novice counselors, and to make readily available to all counselors in need.

Chapter 19 is an amusingly written glossary of Counseling Tips from A to Z. It is worth the reading as much for the fun as for the insights. I particularly recommend the definition of the term ZERP FACTOR. I leave you with Zerp, confident that Michael Pastore will take you from here on his magical journey to the camp we all hope to run.

Arthur Sharenow, CCD
Camp Kenwood-Evergreen

ONE

MISTAKES GROWN-UPS ALWAYS MAKE WITH KIDS

1

How To Be
The Worst Counselor On Earth

Welcome to camp!

The summer air is warm; the sky is clear and blue; birds are singing; the lake is shining; the trees stand majestic; the female staff are lithe and lovely; the males are sensitive and handsome—everything is peaceful and perfect and the world seems like a glowing paradise.

Then a remarkable thing happens: the children arrive!

Dozens of children! Busloads of children! Hundreds of children! The children arrive and they bring their magic enthusiasm, their remarkable sincerity, their radiant energy, and their invincible love of fun and freedom. Suddenly, all at once, the counselors must grow light years and become temporary parents. Huge words such as WORK and RESPONSIBILITY leap into the picture. And the paradise—for the counselors, at least—doesn't look a bit like paradise anymore.

The camp counselor, overwhelmed by this dizzying disorientation, is tempted to react by treating children the same way that most of us were treated. Most grown-ups, at home, schools, and summer camp, know nothing better than to use the **Do-it-or-else! Method of Child Control.** This barbaric method may be summarized in one cold sentence:

"Tell the child what to do; if he disobeys you,
   then threaten and punish him."

Unfortunately, many adults mistakenly believe that all that is necessary to convince a child to behave well is to impose, or threaten to impose, harsh punishments. Here are some real-life examples of these punishments that I have seen practiced in schools, after-school programs, and summer camps.

The Rancid Armpit. One child-care worker reported: "Whenever a kid in my group misbehaved, I stuck his nose under my sweaty armpit. This system worked perfectly for three entire days: during this period there was not even one single incident of disobedience, backtalk, or bad behavior. But on the fourth day, the punished child started to lick my armpit—and the other kids exploded with laughter. The whole system broke down. After that, I couldn't control them."

The Royal Flush. Immediately after doing something wrong, the child is lifted upside-down by his feet, then deposited head-first into the toilet bowl. The gurgle of the flushing toilet is usually loud enough to drown his screams.

The Super-Wedgie. The child is lifted up by the back of his underwear and hung, like a picture, on a hook or nail on the cabin wall. Here he writhes helplessly, like a pinned insect, until his underpants stretch, then tear; and finally he falls—naked and ashamed—onto the hard wood floor.

Rock Patrol. The child is commanded to: "Go out to the softball field and pick up every rock, pebble, and stone! Then, lay these stones on the field to spell out the sentence:
    'I WILL NEVER AGAIN DISOBEY MY COUNSELOR, WHO IS A GREAT HUMAN BEING, EVEN THOUGH HE'S MAKING ME PICK UP ALL THESE LOUSY ROCKS!' "

Midnight Express. Two counselors are needed for this activity. Played at midnight or the wee hours of the early morning, while the camper is sleeping. One counselor shines a bright flashlight beam into the camper's face and makes the roaring sounds of a speeding locomotive. The other counselor shakes the camper vigorously and shouts: "TRAIN COMING!"

The G.E. Special. A kid who won't go to sleep at bedtime is made to stand up under a high-intensity 200-watt lightbulb in the bathroom, until he begs, beseeches, and implores you to be allowed to return to his bed.

Mosquito Party. Dressed in nothing but a bathing suit, the child who caused the most trouble during the day is taken outside of the cabin in the evening, and made to sit on the picnic table. The counselor pours one gallon of "bug juice" (a high-sugar, artificially colored and flavored, nutritionless drink) all over the child's arms and legs. The child is allowed to return to the cabin after he gets 20 mosquito bites, or 3 bee stings—whichever comes first.

LBP: Latrine Beautification Project. The sun rises red over the mountains and a fanfare of trumpets bellow majestically. The door to the outdoor latrine is slowly and reverently pulled open. A sign on the latrine door says, "Room 101". Beneath the sign is the famous quote from Dante: "Abandon all hope ye who enter here." The nauseating stench oozing from the latrine is beyond description. It reeks like sulphur, rotten eggs, dead skunks, male cat spray, and decomposing snails. Shakespeare envisioned this latrine with the poetic words: "The rankest compound of villainous smell that ever offended nostril."

Into this hellish miasma the disobedient camper is thrown. The door is slammed, locked, and bolted behind him. He carries nothing but a bandanna to tie around his face; a plastic bucket; a sponge the size of a 3-by-5 card; a water hose; and a bottle of Pine-Away brand extra-strength antiseptic cleaner. Gagging, choking, and wiping the tears from his eyes, the revolting camper cleans diligently, inspired by the thought that he shall never be released until the dung-encrusted outhouse shines like the throne room of a king.

Using the *Do-it-or-else! Method of Child Control* is the easiest way to become the worst counselor on Earth. Why is this method so common? Because most grown-ups do not understand children and what they need.

Chapter 2 offers a test you can take to assess your counseling skills. This test will reveal how you see and think about children, and help you to teach yourself every important counseling skill you want to learn.

2

Are You A Robot Counselor?
A Self-Evaluation Test

The following passage is taken from the children's novel, *Lark's Magic*. We join the story as a new camp counselor meets his group of children for the first time.

"I'm Milton Cheeseburger, your counselor," the stranger said. "Anybody who makes fun of my name gets a super wedgie."

He was wearing mirrored sunglasses, musky cologne, a turtleneck shirt, polyester tennis shorts, and gold socks under freshly-shined black shoes. He held a box of cinnamon buns in one hand, and a six-pack of soda in the other.

"Are you the brats in bunk one?" Milton said. "You, ugly. Carry my footlockers inside. Put them under the bed with the best mattress. Don't just stand there like a lump of donkey dukey. *Move!*"

Milton was talking to Zerp; Zerp who was wearing a T-shirt saying: 'I'M NOT DEAF, I'M JUST IGNORING YOU'. Zerp scowled and said: "Go jump in the lake three times and come up twice!"

"Hey, *punk!*" the counselor shouted. "You can't talk to *me* like that. I'm your *boss,* do you hear that? Get inside and sit on your bed for the rest of the night!"

"Make me."

"If you say *one more word,*" Milton hollered, pointing a finger at Zerp's face, "your backside is gonna look like maraschino cherries!"

Zerp flashed his cutest smile. "One more word!"

Milton grabbed Zerp around the neck of his T-shirt and dragged him into the cabin. "In college," Milton snapped, "we call this the Royal Flush."

He flipped Zerp upside-down, held his ankles, dropped Zerp's head into the toilet water, and swished him around like a toilet brush.

"We should *do* something!" Lark said, seizing my arm.

"Zerp can handle himself," I said.

Milton pushed down on the metal handle. The gurgles of the flushing water drowned out Zerp's furious shouts.

"Bring those footlockers in here, then sit on your bed, creep!" Milton yelled. "I'm taking a nap for a few hours. The rest of you sapsuckers,"—Milton shot a glance at me and Lark—"can go play on a ledge on the roof of the Empire State Building."

Milton unrolled his sleeping bag on the bed next to the door and climbed inside. He took one bite from a cinnamon bun, two swigs from a soda can, then shut his eyes and fell asleep.

💣

Freeze-the-Action

Get a pencil and a blank sheet of paper and re-read the above passage. At every point where you think that Counselor Cheeseburger has made a mistake (a mistake in something he did, or something he said, or something he failed to do), write a number (first mistake "1", second mistake "2", etc.) on the page. Then number your paper, and explain what the mistake was, and how it could have been handled better.

💣

Attack Of The Robot Counselors

Robot counselors and robot grown-ups can be found everywhere. Robot counselors are counselors who attempt to dominate and control the child using force, threats, and punishments.

The effective way to work with children is the way of the Caring Counselor: win the child's trust and cooperation by playing with the child, listening to the child, and giving the child complete sincerity. Robot counselors fail to establish this friendship and rapport. What they cannot accomplish by friendship they try to do by force. And this force always fails, because it creates an unhappy, unfree, and emotionally unhealthy child.

Are you a Robot Counselor? How good are your counseling skills? Find out by taking the *Camp Counselor Self-Evaluation Test* on page 8 and page 9. The answers to the test are given on page 26.

Camp Counselor Self-Evaluation Test Part 1

Instructions. After each sentence 1 to 25, write in the **one** letter (either A, O, S, R, or N) that matches most closely with your opinion. Draw an asterisk (*) next to the statements that you think are tricky or difficult.
Optional: If you want to clarify or explain any of your answers, then use additional sheets of paper.
KEY: A = Always or Very Often O = Often S = Sometimes
     R = Rarely N = Never

1. Since people get what they expect, the counselor should expect perfect behavior from his/her campers.

2. It is O.K. to scream or yell at children when you are angry with them for something wrong that they did.

3. If a child throws food in the dining hall, then to teach him to behave better it is a good idea to take away his dessert.

4. Counselors should praise children, either in words or with notes.

5. You get kids to do their best by encouraging a strong feeling of individual competition among kids in the cabin group.

6. Counselors should lead their group of kids to play games, share nature, and sing and chant.

7. A good way to motivate children is to promise them money or material things if they do a good job.

8. Every day, the counselor should spend a few minutes talking one-to-one with each camper.

9. The counselor will lose his authority and be unable to control the children if he plays games with the children.

10. When a child needs it or deserves it, a counselor should shove, push, grab, or gently hit the child.

Camp Counselor Self-Evaluation Test Part 2

11. Children need special attention at bedtime.	
12. If the child misbehaves, then the counselor should speak to the child in a calm and friendly voice.	
13. A counselor should listen very carefully to what a child says.	
14. The counselor should let children make some of the decisions about how they want to spend their time.	
15. It's O.K. to talk about a child's misbehavior in front of other children.	
16. If 2 kids in a group misbehave, you should punish the whole group to make sure that the misbehavior never happens again.	
17. You are playing a card game with a nine-year-old-child. Should you play your best and try to win?	
18. It is O.K. to threaten a child with a harsh punishment, as long as you never carry out the threat.	
19. If you do threaten a child with harsh punishment, you should carry out the threat so that the child will listen to you.	
20. When a child is causing trouble, the counselor should tell him: "If you keep on being bad, you will be sent home."	
21. Children misbehave when you give them freedom.	
22. Adults should lie to children or deceive children in order to protect them and to get them to obey us.	
23. Watching television and playing electronic video games are entertaining and beneficial ways for children to spend their time.	
24. Adults can learn many important things from children.	
25. Children must be allowed to develop freely and to create their own values.	

3

You're Ugly & Your Mother Dresses You Funny: More Mistakes Most Grown-ups Make

In a wonderful book titled *Growing Young,* anthropologist Ashley Montagu—the Socrates of the modern world—describes the importance of what he calls *sound thinking.* We must learn how to think soundly, Montagu believes, because unsound thinking leads us to unsound behavior—actions that are harmful to ourselves and others.

Why do grown-ups make so many mistakes with kids? The answer is simple and profound: Because we have inherited so many unsound ideas about children. Instead of trying to understand children and giving children what they need, we make demands on children and punish them when they fail to fulfill our unreasonable demands. Instead of creating unique and fresh ideas from our own minds, we buy the same old tasteless canned ideas that everybody else buys.

Here are the four outmoded and canned beliefs that cause the most mistakes in the way grown-ups behave toward kids.

Canned Belief # 1: Children need to be controlled by force and punishments.

The complete opposite is true. Using force and punishments never works in the long run, and always harms the child.

Caring grown-ups never attempt to control children. Instead, we win the child's cooperation and respect. When the child likes, respects, and admires the grown-up, then grown-up and child will work harmoniously together. Our children will be free from unhealthy fears, and become self-reliant human beings. And they will listen to us because they love and trust our leadership, instead of fearing our threats and punishments.

Canned Belief # 2: For the child's own good, grown-ups should lie to the child.

Telling a lie to a child, or deceiving a child, is a grave mistake, because it hinders the intellectual and emotional development of the child. Truth can be told to children: in the book *Summerhill, A Radical Approach To Child Rearing,* A.S. Neill states that in 38 years he never consciously told a lie to any of his pupils.

The justifiable exception is when a lie protects a life in danger. The other exception is when 9-year-old Mary asks: "Who do you like better, me or Ann?"

Telling Mary the truth, that I like Ann better, would be emotionally crushing. In this case I answer: "I treat everyone equally and I like everyone the same amount." Mary, who wants to hear that you like her more than anyone else in the Universe, may not be thrilled with the answer—but it's the best you can do. If you demonstrate with your actions that you like her, she will be satisfied.

Of course, if there are subjects that you do not want to talk about, just say so. When boys or girls ask you to tell them graphic details about your current sex life, you can truthfully answer: "That's too personal. I don't want to tell you."

Canned Belief # 3: Giving freedom to children is dangerous.

The complete opposite is true. Freedom is absolutely necessary for the healthy development of the child.

Freedom is an essential condition for love. Children raised in an atmosphere of freedom will learn to love life, love their work, and love other human beings.

Adults should be "the boss" in all matters that involve the child's health and safety, but children should be free to make most other decisions in their lives.

Canned Belief # 4: Adults should not be friends with children.

Another false and harmful belief. Many adults worry that if they become "too friendly" with children, the children will lose their fear of them and fail to obey. Some people mistakenly call this fear "respect"—but genuine respect can only be won by kindness, never by force. When children fear a grown-up they will hate the grown-up, and they will not behave well when the grown-up is not around.

This theory, canned belief # 4, works for training dogs and armies, but not for children. To work effectively with children, the grown-up must establish a warm and sincere friendship with the child. Chapters 4 through 19 in this book describe the many things that counselors can do to establish and maintain this friendship.

King Of The Kreeps

The following exercise, KING OF THE KREEPS, is designed to help us to remember the mistakes that grown-ups always make, and to remember how painful they can be to the children involved. This exercise can be worked on alone by the reader (with a pencil and paper); or it can be used as the basis for a discussion, in groups of 2 to 6 persons.

Instructions: You are going to create three King (or Queen) Kreeps named King (or Queen) Bigmouth, King (or Queen) Blunderful, and King (or Queen) Duzznuthin.

To create these characters, use your own experiences, and the experiences of children and people you know. Use the fiction writer's trick of making a *composite character:* your perfect Kreep may be the combination of worst qualities from many persons you know. Your King (or Queen) Bigmouth may have your English teacher's sarcastic scowl, your grandmother's nagging voice, the unabashed arrogance of a waiter at a fine dining establishment, and so on.

CREATING KING BIGMOUTH OR QUEEN BIGMOUTH

1. What does this King/Queen Bigmouth look like? Describe face, eyes, body, gestures, tone of voice. Pretend that you are describing this person to someone who cannot see the KREEP because they are separated from the KREEP by a high stone wall.

2. Bigmouth's big mistakes are these: Bigmouth says things to children that he should not say. Write down the letters A, B, and C and after each letter write something Bigmouth always says to children that should not be said.

3. For each of your ideas in A, B, and C, answer the question: Why is it a mistake to say this to a child?

4. For each of your ideas in A, B, and C, answer the question: How might the child feel if someone said this to him or her?

5. For each of your ideas, answer: What are alternatives to these statements? In other words: What could the counselor say instead of the things that Bigmouth always says?

CREATING KING BLUNDERFUL OR QUEEN BLUNDERFUL

1. Describe the physical characteristics of King/Queen Blunderful.

2. Blunderful's mistakes are mistakes of action. Write down the letters A, B, and C and after each letter write something Blunderful might DO to children that he should not do. When answering this question, write down all the mistakes that you can think of **except** mistakes where the grown-up uses harsh punishments, like the ones described in Chapter 1.

3. For each of your ideas in A, B, and C, answer the question: Why is it a mistake to do this to a child?

4. For each of your ideas in A, B, and C, answer the question: How might the child feel if a grown-up did this to him or her?

5. For each of your ideas, answer: What are alternatives to these actions? In other words: What could the counselor do instead of the things that Blunderful always does?

CREATING KING DUZZNUTHIN OR QUEEN DUZZNUTHIN

1. Describe the physical characteristics of King/Queen Duzznuthin.

2. Duzznuthin's big mistakes are these: Duzznuthin never does for children things that he should do. Write down the letters A, B, and C and after each letter write something Duzznuthin never does for children, something that he should be doing.

3. For each of your ideas in A, B, and C, answer the question: Why is it a mistake not to do this for a child?

4. For each of your ideas in A, B, and C, answer the question: How might the child feel if a grown-up failed to do what Duzznuthin never did?

5. For each of your ideas, answer: What are alternatives to this inaction? In other words: Write down three or more things that counselors should always do for kids.

The Deadly Dozen:
The 12 Most Common Child-Maintenance Mistakes

Here are the twelve most common mistakes that destroy relationships between adults and children. Compare these mistakes with the ones you have described in your answers to King Bigmouth & Queen Blunderful. DO NOT SAY and DO NOT DO any of the following things to the children you live with or work with.

Why not? ...

Because, after working with thousands of children, we have observed that saying and doing these things makes the child more angry, more frustrated, more unhappy. Children misbehave because they are unhappy. And the unhappier the child is, the more he or she will misbehave.

1. DO NOT utilize the Do-it-or-else! Method of Child Control. In other words: do not use force, threats, intimidations, or punishments. DO NOT PUNISH children: TEACH them.

☠

2. DO NOT scream or yell at children. When anger is directed at children, this anger crushes their self-esteem. When you become angry, first calm yourself down before you talk with the child.

☠

3. DO NOT attempt to intimidate or bully children by using the language of guilt and fear. DO NOT tell children that they are bad. If Zerp punches Joey, then instead of saying: "You are **bad**!" or "What you did was **bad**!", tell Zerp the simple fact: "What you did hurt Joey."   Your words to children are either weapons or gifts. If you hurt a child's feelings, he will never forget it, he will never forgive you, he will never respect you.

☠

4. DO NOT lie to the child and do not deceive the child. The three rules for working with children are: Be sincere; Be sincere; Be sincere.

5. DO NOT try to change the child or mold the child. Let children be free to grow and develop in their own unique ways. Do not try to change the child's behavior unless you first ask yourself if the child's behavior is hurting himself or another human being. (See Chapter 19: Freedom, not License.)

☠

6. DO NOT hurt the child's feelings. Do NOT label children. DO NOT call children names. If you say something like "You are a troublemaker!", then the child will be so upset he will make ten times as much trouble as before.

☠

7. DO NOT act like a Robot Grown-up: Present in Body, Absent in Mind. Children need the presence of grown-ups who enjoy being with them, enjoy playing with them, enjoy teaching them, and enjoy learning from them.

☠

8. DO NOT be an archaeologist and dig up the past: do not remind the misbehaving child what he did wrong yesterday or the day before.

☠

9. DO NOT try to lecture a child when he is upset. First, let him alone to calm down; or talk soothingly to him until he calms down.

☠

10. DO NOT talk about a child's misbehavior in front of other children.

☠

11. DO NOT punish the whole group for the misbehavior of one or two persons.

☠

12. DO NOT be afraid to say NO. Say NO to the child whenever he is hurting himself or hurting another child or living thing. Say NO whenever the child interferes with the freedom of another child.

TWO

HOW TO UNDERSTAND CHILDREN
&
HOW TO GIVE CHILDREN
WHAT THEY NEED

Introduction

The child's success or failure at camp depends, more than anything else, on the relationship between the child and the counselor. Whenever the counselor is cold, apathetic, or tyrannical then—even if the rest of camp is a paradise—we find unhappy children. Whenever the counselor is caring, enthusiastic, and sincere—even if the camp is nothing more than a picnic table on a scrap of neglected land—children return home glowing with magical experiences and unforgettable memories.

In the previous chapters we examined the ways of the Robot Counselors. Robot Counselors are counselors who attempt to dominate and control the child; persons who are not childlike enough to live fully in the present moment and enjoy being with and playing with kids.

The entire remainder of this book is devoted to helping you to understand what it means to be a **Caring** Counselor. Caring Counselors are childlike human beings who love being with children. Caring Counselors treat the child as an equal and as a friend: with love, sincerity, and trust.

The Caring Counselor relates harmoniously with the child because she understands what children need and how to give it to them. In addition to the basic need for an environment that allows them to be safe and healthy, the six most important needs of children are:

1. The need to love and to be loved
2. The need to play
3. The need for Freedom to develop in their own unique way
4. The need to live in and play in Nature
5. The need to do creative activities and the arts
6. The need to learn and the need to learn how to think and make decisions

Throughout Chapters 4, 5, & 6 we explore these and other important themes.

The Martian From Jupiter:
Glimpses Of The Nature Of The Child

"Other planets are speeding away from the earth at the rate of millions of miles per hour. Who can blame them?"

—Hieronymus Anonymous

A Martian from Jupiter—a remarkably intelligent creature—has surveyed all of planet Earth's literature and philosophy. With the help of a supercomputer smaller than a jellybean, he has compiled a list of the 32 wisest statements about children and child management.

Fill in the blank with the letter or double-letter of the answer that belongs there. Answers can be found on page 26.

A. acceptance	B. angry	C. changed	D. dangerous
E. deserve	F. education	G. enthusiasm	H. example
I. artist	J. heart	K. imitate	L. kids
M. life	N. lovingly	O. models	P. play
Q. power	R. present	S. problems	T. respond
U. symptom	V. time	W. trust	X. unhappy
Y. yourself	Z. sincere	AA. love	BB. child
CC. alternatives	DD. respect	EE. believing	FF. giving

1. The difficult child is the child who is _____. He is at war with himself; and in consequence he is at war with the whole world. (A.S. Neill).

2. If a child lives with _____ , he learns to like himself. (D. Nolte)

3. Children have more need of _____ than of critics. (Joseph Joubert)

4. Children need love, especially when they do not _____ it. (H.S. Hulbert).

5. Too often we give children answers to remember rather than _____ to solve. (R.Lewin).

6. Every child is an _____. The problem is how to remain an _____ once he grows up. (Picasso).

7. Children think not of the past, nor what is to come, but enjoy the _____ time, which few of us do. (Jean de la Bruyere).

8. The meaning of life is to live as if ____ and love were one. (Montagu)

9. The future of mankind depends on the _____ of children. (Aristotle)

10. You can only love a child if you become a child _____ . (A.S. Neill)

11. Teaching by _____ is not the main way to teach. It is the only way. (A. Schweitzer)

12. _____ is like holding an egg in your hand. If you hold too tightly, you crush the egg; if you hold too loosely, you drop the egg and it breaks. (African proverb)

13. Whenever a child lies you will always find a severe parent. A lie would have no sense unless the truth were felt to be _____. (Alfred Adler).

14. The truth must be spoken _____ . (Thoreau)

15. A human being should always _____ , but never react. (A. Montagu)

16. You can do anything with children if only you ____ with them. (Prince Otto von Bismarck).

17. If you want to help people, don't get _____ with them. (Kalahari bushman)

18. We must have a place where children can have a whole group of adults they can _____ . (Margaret Mead)

19. If there is anything we wish to change in the child, we should first examine it and see whether it is not something that could be better _____ in ourselves. (Carl Jung).

20. Every boy, in his _____, would rather steal second base than an automobile. (Tom Clark)

21. There are three ways to get something done: do it yourself; hire someone to do it; or forbid your _____ to do it. (Hieronymous Anonymous)

22. In bringing up children, spend half as much money, and twice as much _____. (H.S. Hulbert).

23. Children have never been very good at listening to their elders, but they have never failed to _____ them. (James Baldwin).

24. Do not mistake a child for his _____ . (Erik Erikson).

25. Children are remarkable for their intelligence and _____, for their curiosity, their intolerance of shams, the clarity and ruthlessness of their vision. (Aldous Huxley).

26. The three most important rules for working with children are: Be sincere; Be sincere; and Be _____. (Michael Pastore).

27. What is hell? I believe it is the suffering caused by the inability to _____. (Dostoyevsky).

28. Inside every man is a _____, an animal, an artist, and a saint. (Emerson)

29. I don't give advice; all I do is set before you the _____. (A.S. Neill)

30. You must teach your children that the ground beneath their feet is the ashes of our grandfathers. So that they will _____ the land, tell your children that the earth is rich with the lives of our kin. Teach your children what we have taught our children, that the earth is our mother. Whatever befalls the earth befalls the sons of the earth. If men spit upon the ground, they spit upon themselves. (American Indian)

31. It is by _____ in roses that we bring them to bloom. (French proverb)

32. The only meaningful way of life is activity in the world; not activity in general but the activity of _____ and caring for fellow creatures. (Fromm)

5

How To Give Children What They Need: The 10 Basic Principles Of Child Maintenance

The Caring Counselor practices these ten basic principles in order to establish a warm friendship and sincere rapport with each child. The counselor who transforms these principles into loving actions wins the child's trust, respect, and cooperation. More importantly, the counselor helps to create a free and happy child.

Read the ten statements below, then pick out the one that is the most interesting to you. Answer, in writing or in group discussion, these questions: What does this statement mean to you? Why do you think that it is important?

1. **RESPECT** the child. Children respond according to the way they are treated. Respect the child by **never** using force, threats, or punishments against the child.

2. Establish a warm **FRIENDSHIP** with each child by being childlike and sincere. The grown-up must establish a warm, playful, and trusting friendship with each child.

3. **LISTEN** to the child with complete acceptance. Each child needs one grown-up who understands how to listen with sincerity, listen with approval, and listen with complete acceptance of the child's feelings.

4. **PLAY** with the child. Children and grown-ups become friends when they play together.

5. Give the child **FREEDOM** but not License. Children become unique and self-reliant human beings only when they are given freedom to make decisions.

6. Share **NATURE** with the child. Children who live and play in nature will learn reverence for all living things.

7. Do **CREATIVE ACTIVITIES** with the child. By doing creative activities instead of passively watching TV, the child develops her mind, her imagination, her whole self.

8. Teach children **HOW TO THINK**. Children need to learn how to think, not what to think. Teach children how to think by giving children problems to solve, great books to read, the chance to explore their interests, and the opportunity to discuss issues that they feel are interesting and important.

9. Respond **NON-AGGRESSIVELY** to a child's misbehavior. Respond non-aggressively and lovingly to a child's misbehavior by letting the child help you to solve the problem. Calmly listen and talk with the child; discuss respect for living things; and use the WE TECHNIQUE. (See Chapter 19).

10. Give **LOVE-ENERGY** to children in **all** moments. Give love-energy to children in **all** moments, *especially* when children withdraw or misbehave. A child's aggression, passiveness, personal problems, or difficult misbehaviors can be healed in this way: love the child, play with the child, talk with the child, and listen to the child.

6

Inside The Child:
How To Use Empathy To Understand
Children's Feelings And Needs

Could a greater miracle take place than for us to look
through each other's eyes for an instant?
                                    —Thoreau, *Journals*

EMPATHY means "feeling-in"; it is the ability to step inside the heart and mind
of another human being. When we use empathy we understand another person
so deeply that their thoughts, motives and feelings are vivid and clear to us.
When you empathize with me, you see what I see; you feel what I feel.

Without using empathy we cannot listen to children, we cannot understand
children, we cannot appreciate children. If Seymour steals my favorite rubber
duckie, my first thought might be: "Damn that sneaky Seymour! I'll get him for
this!". But if—by using empathy—I realize **why** Seymour stole the duckie (maybe
his father beats him when he plays with his father's duckie), then instantaneously
I leap light-years closer to the solution of Seymour's situation. Now I can try to
treat the **cause** of Seymour's misbehavior. And I feel kinder and more
compassionate toward Seymour, as well.

Use the Empathy Game to teach yourself this essential idea: When children
misbehave they do not need our anger and punishment. At all times, children
need our wisdom, sincerity, and kindness.

The Empathy Game

Look at each of the following ten situations, and pick out the ones that are the
most interesting to you. Then use empathy to imagine and appreciate how
it would feel to be a specific child in this specific situation. After thinking about
and feeling about the situation, write down the answer to the questions A to D.

A) What would the child be thinking about and feeling in this situation?
B) What things might a child in this situation do, and why?
C) If you were the child in this situation, what things could a counselor say to you that would make you feel better?
D) If you were the child in this situation, what things could a counselor do for you that would help you?

1. YOUR FIRST MOMENT AT CAMP. You are a child who arrives at camp for the first time, and is meeting the counselor and the other children for the first time.

2. VERY SHY. You are a child so shy that you are not talking to the counselor or other kids.

3. HATES SWIMMING. You are a child who will not put his head under water at swimming time.

4. HOMESICK. You are a child who misses home very much.

5. SCREAMING DAD. You are a child who tells his counselor: "My father yells at my mom all the time. I think he's crazy."

6. BUTTERFINGERS. You are Sam, who has been put into right field and nicknamed "Butterfingers". You have just dropped an easy fly ball that allows the other team to score 3 runs and win the game in the bottom of the 9th inning.

7. IT COULD HAPPEN TO YOU. You are a child who has just seen a video about Lyme Disease, and now you are unusually quiet.

8. HUMAN TARGET. You are a child who is being teased by the other kids in the cabin.

9. THE FIGHTER. You are a child who has just gotten into a fistfight with a child from another cabin.

10. NO MONEY. You are a child from a poor family who cannot afford to buy anything (ice cream, soda, souvenirs) from the camp store.

ANSWERS TO COUNSELING TESTS & MARTIAN FROM JUPITER

Answers to Martian from Jupiter (from page 19)

1=X; 2=A; 3=O; 4=E; 5=S; 6=I; 7=R; 8=M; 9=F; 10=Y;
11=H; 12=Q; 13=D; 14=N; 15=T; 16=P; 17=B; 18=W;
19=C; 20=J; 21=L; 22=V; 23=K; 24=U; 25=G; 26=Z;
27=AA; 28=BB; 29=CC; 30=DD; 31=EE; 32=FF.

Answers to Counselor Self-Evaluation Test Part 1 (from page 8)

1=N; 2=N; 3=N; 4=A; 5=N; 6=A; 7=N; 8=A; 9=N; 10=N;

Answers to Counselor Self-Evaluation Test Part 2 (from page 9)

11=A; 12=A; 13=A; 14=A; 15=R; 16=N; 17=S; 18=N; 19=N;
20=N; 21=R or N are both correct; 22=N; 23=N; 24=A; 25=A.

Scoring for Camp Counselor Self-Evaluation Tests

Score 8 points for each correct answer, zero points for incorrect answers.
Add up your combined total points from Part 1 and Part 2.

200 to 184 points:	Excellent
176 to 164 points:	Very Good
156 to 144 points:	Good
136 to 120 points:	Average
112 to 96 points:	Below Average
88 points or less:	Oil your joints! You are a Robot Counselor!

Whatever your score, you can improve your counseling skills by study and practice. All the themes relating to these questions are explained in various chapters of this book, and in the book *Zen In The Art Of Child Maintenance*.

THREE

WHAT GREAT COUNSELORS DO

7

What's It Really Like?
One Day In The Life
Of A Camp Counselor

What is the life of a camp counselor really like?

One thing that life at camp is *not* like is the way it is portrayed on the movie screen. Hollywood counselors, in movies such as TOFUBALLS, are shown as lazy and self-serving pranksters, with nothing on their minds except food and the pursuit of the opposite sex—but not in that order. Hollywood camps are depicted as completely chaotic, unplanned, and unsupervised. And Hollywood Camp Directors are made out to be thoroughly incompetent boobs who hire sex maniacs for staff and know absolutely nothing about what happens at the camp.

Nothing—almost nothing—could be further from the reality.

The truth is that most camps are extremely well organized, most camp directors are competent professionals, and most counselors come to camp to put the needs of the children first. **Camp counseling is hard work.** Extremely hard work. Rewarding work, with lots of fun and friendship, and priceless memories—but hard work all the same. The counselors who get the most from camp are the counselors who get their happiness from giving: giving of themselves, sharing, making other persons happy, helping children to learn and grow.

Chapters 7 and 8 explain in great detail what a typical camp day is like, what the counselor's job is, and what things great counselors always do.

We begin with a look at the daily schedule from Camp Runarunamuckmuck, a typical children's resident (overnight) camp. On the page after is a minute-by-minute account of what the counselors would be doing during that busy schedule.

1993 Camp Runarunamuckmuck Daily Schedule		
TIME	PLACE	ACTIVITY
7:00	Cabin	RISING BELL and WAKE UP
7:00-7:45	Cabin Area	WASH UP
7:50-8:00	Flagpole	FLAG RAISING & GOOD MORNINGS
8:00-8:30	Lodge	BREAKFAST
8:30-9:00	In Cabin	CLEANUP & CABIN MEETING
9:00-9:10	Cabin Areas	Unit Meetings (for Staff)
9:15-10:15	Activity Area	ACTIVITY 1: Arts, Nature, Sports, H_2O
10:15-11:15	Activity Area	ACTIVITY 2: Arts, Nature, Sports, H_2O
11:15-12:15	Various places	Supervised FREE TIME
12:00-12:15	Lodge	Lunch Set Up for scheduled cabins
12:15-1:00	Lodge	LUNCH and SINGING
1:00-2:00	In Cabin	REST HOUR
2:00-3:00	Activity Area	ACTIVITY 3: Arts, Nature, Sports, H_2O
3:00-3:30	Picnic Area	SNACK & BOARD GAMES
3:30-4:30	Activity Area	ACTIVITY 4: Arts, Nature, Sports, H_2O
4:30-5:30	with your own cabin of kids	CABIN TIME 1. Counselors play any game that their kids choose.
5:15-6:30	Lodge	Dinner Set Up then DINNER
6:30-7:30	Various Places	SURPRISE HOUR
7:30-8:00	Flagpole	Flag lowering & time-for-thought
8:00-9:00	Amphitheater	EVENING PROGRAM
9:00-10:00	In Cabin	CABIN TIME 2 Counselors talk or read stories to kids. Lights out 10 P.M.

CAMP RUNARUNAMUCKMUCK
DAILY SCHEDULE PROCEDURES FOR COUNSELORS

And where is the humble camp counselor during this lightning-paced frenzy of frolic and fun? Many a camp director has asked this very question. The answer is typified in the detailed description below.

Many camps—and Runarunamuckmuck is one of them—require the counselor to do two jobs in one. One part of the job, and in my opinion the most important one, is to live and work with the children in his or her cabin group. Counselors usually live in a cabin with six to eight children. Sometimes a co-counselor is assigned to help; other times a "junior staff" (age 14 to 17) is your assistant; and often you fly alone. Counselors wake up their group, eat meals with the kids, put them to sleep, play games with the kids, and act as a mom, dad, big brother or sister, and best friend all rolled into one.

Another facet of the counselor's job is to teach or assist in one of the four program areas: Art, Nature, Sports, or Waterfront. Counselors choose, or are assigned, an area where they have a strong skill or interest. In the Runarunamuckmuck world, the counselor works as an instructor or a program assistant during the four activity periods, for four hours per day. Here he or she gets the chance to meet and work with all the other children in the camp.

7:00   Rising Bell. Wake up promptly and gently wake up your campers. If your group is scheduled for shower time now, then take them to the showers; if not, make sure your campers wash face and hands and change clothes.

7:50   Assemble At Flagpole. Make sure that all of your campers and junior staff are present at Flag Raising. Walk together to the flagpole as a group. Look at each child and see if anyone looks ill, troubled, sad, upset, or homesick.

8:00   Breakfast. Sit with your cabin of kids and your junior staff assistant. Help the kids to get the food. The counselor is responsible for ensuring that not more than one person at a time gets up from the table. DO NOT allow food to be thrown. After the meal, clean the table and floor. Ask the Head Counselor if your group can leave. Make sure kids who need medication visit the nurse.

8:30   Clean Up. Make sure your cabin does their Cabin Clean-up and Cabin Duties: see chart on wall for list.

8:50   Cabin Meetings. The counselor leads a cabin meeting with all the kids. At this meeting you review today's schedule, tell jokes, work out group problems, and let the kids vote for what they want to do during Cabin Time I. If your cabin group has swimming in the morning, remind the kids to wear or bring bathing suits and towels. Find out which kids are in specialty camp programs, and remind them to go.

9:00   Staff Meetings. Meet with your Head Counselor and other staff. Make sure your junior staff is with the cabin.

9:10   Leave for activity area: Art, Nature, Sports, or Waterfront. Walk down to program areas with your kids. Sing or chant along the way.

9:15   1st Activity Period. Counselors in the program areas should be *actively* involved with the kids.

10:15 2nd Activity Period. Counselors in the program areas should be *actively* involved with the kids.

11:15 Supervised Free Time. Be in your assigned area. Play with the kids, or talk with the kids, or (at least) attentively watch the kids.

12:15 Lunch. No more than two counselors should be sitting at one table, because this will cause a "counselor shortage" at other tables. When someone raises their hand to make an announcement, ask kids at your table to be quiet.

1:00   Rest Hour. Counselors are in the cabin with the kids. It is time to nap or read or write. If you are willing sit on the front steps and watch them, then your kids who want to play *quietly* outside may play right outside the cabin.

2:00   3rd Activity Period. Counselors should be *actively* involved with kids.

3:00   Snack and Supervised Free Time. All children and staff are in the "tepee" area, opposite the lodge. Staff should be *actively* involved with children: talk with kids, play quiet games with kids, or watch the kids.

3:30   4th Activity Period. Counselors should be *actively* involved with kids.

4:30   Cabin Time I. Counselors and their kids do an activity that the children have voted on. Need ideas? Find out what the kids want to do, then do it.

5:15   Dinner Set Up for assigned cabins: counselors help the kids set the table.

5:30   Dinner. Eat with your cabin group. Clean table and floor afterwards.

6:20   Dish Duty. Once a week the counselor assists with the dishes.

6:30   Surprise Hour. Be prepared to lead a game or activity.

7:30   Flag Lowering and Time-for-Thought. Stay with your kids at the flag, and walk with them up to Time-for-Thought area.

8:00   Evening Program. One time each week the counselor will be responsible for planning and preparing the program. During evening program, if you're not leading it, sit with your kids, and encourage them to participate in the program. After evening program is over, gather your kids together, check that all are present, then walk back to the cabin with your kids.

9:00   Cabin Time II. Counselors help the kids get ready for bed: all children MUST brush their teeth at this time. Night time is the most important part of the child's day. Staff must spend at least 45 minutes, from 9:15 to about 10 P.M., talking with the children. Talk quietly, sing quietly with guitar, or read stories. Leading a group discussion is one of the best ways to use this time. Talk about the fun you had today; and make plans for tomorrow.

10:00 Staff time off. Unless you have night duty or you and your kids are overnight camping, you will probably be off between 10 P.M. and midnight. Staff free time begins at 10 P.M., or later if your kids are not quiet and settled down.

12:00 Staff Curfew. All staff must be back and inside their cabins.

Exhausted from just reading about it?   At many camps, and at all camps accredited by the American Camping Association, staff members have 2 hours off per day, somewhere between the hours of 7 A.M. and midnight. In addition, counselors usually get 24 hours off per seven-day week.

Catch your breath and turn to Chapter 8, where we begin to think about what it takes to be a great counselor.

8

The Secrets Of Working With Children

CREATING THE CARING COUNSELOR

In this exercise, the opposite of King of the Kreeps, you will create a Caring Camp Counselor. Make the best counselor by using, as a model, a real person or an ideal figment of your imagination.

1. Describe the physical features of the best camp counselor you know, or the best camp counselor you can imagine.

2. Write down three key words or phrases that describe this caring counselor.

3. What human-relations skills would this caring counselor have?

4. Write three sentences that this caring counselor would say to kids.

5. Write down three things that this counselor would do with his kids, or do for his kids.

6. What things would this caring counselor do to make his/her group of children feel close together like a team, and like a family?

7. How does this counselor respond when children misbehave?

8. What does this counselor do to prevent a child's misbehavior?

9. Does this counselor enjoy his/her work? Why or why not?

10. Write down three or more characteristics, qualities, or actions of a great counselor.

The Secrets Of Working With Children: 10 Things Caring Counselors Always Do

Everyone says: "I love kids!"; but if you really love children then you will demonstrate that love by your ACTIONS. This love-energy, communicated by these loving actions, transforms and deepens the friendship between the counselor and the child. The secret of working with children is to establish a warm friendship with the child. To accomplish this, Caring Counselors do these things:

Action	Description
1. Make safety and health the number one priority.	Caring Counselors are with their children, or know where their children are, at all times. Caring Counselors say a calm and friendly "No!" to children whenever children are hurting themselves, hurting other children, or hurting living things.
2. Play with the kids.	Caring Counselors are always found with their group of children, watching them, listening to them, playing with them, having fun together.
3. Listen to children and have one-to-one talks with each child.	Because each child needs special individual attention, Caring Counselors make time for one-to-one talks with each child every day. Listen deeply, and let the child do most of the talking.
4. Create enthusiasm.	Create enthusiasm by singing, chanting, laughing, being cheerful, being enthusiastic, and genuinely enjoying being with the kids.
5. Praise and encourage children.	Praise the child whenever she does something creative, altruistic, unselfish, or beneficial for the whole group. Use spoken words or special notes. Children need praise and encouragement like flowers need water and sunshine.

6. Lead children, but never boss them.	Caring Counselors are not bosses, they are leaders. • The boss says "I"; the leader says "We." • The boss inspires fear; the leader inspires enthusiasm. • The boss shouts: "Do it!"; the leader says "Let's do it together." • The boss makes work a drudgery; the leader makes it a game.
7. Meet every day with your group of kids.	Caring Counselors lead daily meetings with their kids, to share experiences, laugh together, discuss problems, make plans. This is the time to let children make decisions, and talk about whatever topics are the most interesting to them.
8. Stay alert for children who need extra help.	Caring Counselors are continuously on the watch for children who are unhappy and having problems. Children who are too aggressive or too quiet usually need extra special attention. Encourage children to talk but never force them.
9. Put the needs of the children first.	To work effectively with children you must put the needs of your group of children ahead of your own personal needs. Examples: Let the children decide what they want to do at cabin time, don't reject ideas because they are too much trouble for you. Serve children first at meals. During the work day, you should be interacting primarily with the children: the time to chat with your staff friends is during your free time. Your happiness at camp should come primarily from giving and sharing with others.
10. Give special attention to each child at bedtime.	When the children are in bed, read or tell stories, sing quiet songs, or lead informal discussions with the kids. At this time, give a few moments of one-to-one attention to each child.

COUNSELING HINTS: HOW TO CREATE INSTANT ENTHUSIASM

You can create instant enthusiasm, with any size group of children, at any time of day or night, by leading one of these four simple activities.

1. The Energy Cheer. To give a rousing Energy Cheer, huddle with your kids in a close circle; stick your hands on top of one another's hands; then, as loudly as you can, shout: "HOORAY!!!". Any other words or phrases may be shouted, as long as you shout them with superabundant enthusiasm.

2. The SuperHug. Give yourselves a SuperHug by huddling together in a circle, then counting down: "3 ... 2 ... 1 ... NOW!". On "NOW!", crush each other in an embrace as powerful as a python.

3. The Hug Monster is a swarm of children who chase someone—an adult or a child—then crush them inside a SuperHug. To start the game, the counselor blows a whistle then yells: "Hug Monster on ... the Camp Director!"—and the pack of laughing children charge toward the flabbergasted prey.

4. Singing and Chanting. A summer camp without singing is like a hole without the donut. Counselors and kids should sing all the time: the more you sing the better you feel. If kids are shy about singing, start with the chants—which are technically defined as loud noises somewhere between shouts and songs. We will start you off with the never-published-before **Pizza Chant.**

Kids (and grown-ups) love this one. Sing it at least 3 times, and go faster and faster and faster each time around. The leader chants the first line and the kids repeat the same words the leader chanted.

Counselor: Eat!	Kids repeat: Eat!
Counselor: Eat a!	Kids repeat: Eat a!
Counselor: Eat a lot!	Kids repeat: Eat a lot!
Counselor: Pizza!	Kids repeat: Pizza!

Counselor: Eat a lotta, eat a lotta, eat a lotta pizza!
Kids repeat: Eat a lotta, eat a lotta, eat a lotta pizza!
Counselor: No, no don't eat the pizza!
Kids repeat: No, no don't eat the pizza!
Counselor: Pizza's got a lotta hotta spicy pepperoni on it, got a lotta hotta pepperoni on the top!
Kids repeat: Pizza's got a lotta hotta spicy pepperoni on it, got a lotta hotta pepperoni on the top!

FOUR

HOW TO PLAY
&
HAVE FUN WITH THE KIDS

9

BREAKING THE ICE:
How To Play 16
Getting Acquainted Games (GAGs)

GAGs—Getting Acquainted Games—are games you can use to introduce children to you and to each other. Start the kids playing as soon as possible after they arrive at camp.

1. UpBall. In addition to being tremendously fun, this is a great game for building cooperation and teamwork. The ball should be a beach ball, or (even better) the soccer-ball-sized light plastic play-balls sold in supermarkets. With younger children, use a balloon instead of a ball. To play, stand in a circle. All the players play together, against a common opponent: Doctor Gravity. The object of the game is to hit the ball, keep the ball in the air, and NOT to let the ball hit the ground. When the ball hits the ground the round is over and you start a new round. Count each time you hit the ball as 1 point, and see how many points you can get. One player may hit the ball no more that three times in a row. The ball may be hit by *any* part of your body. Play on a big grassy field, with lots of room to run.

2. Introducing. Divide the group into teams of two partners. Make sure that the partners have not met before, or do not know each other very well. For three minutes, partner 1 tells partner 2 all about himself. Then partner 2 must tell the whole group all about partner 1 (for 30 seconds). After all the partner 1s have been introduced, the partner 2s tell partner 1s about themselves, and partner 2 tells the group all about partner 1. Use a watch with a timer to keep things moving along.

3. Pick Yourself Up. Divide the group into teams of two partners. Partners sit on the ground, turn back-to-back (touching each other), then lock their arms. The object of the game is to stand up together. After this round is finished, make the teams into 3 players, and try again. When 3 players are done, try 4 players, then 5, and so on up to 10 players together. It gets more difficult (and more fun) as you add more people to the group. Try a variation where the players sit down, face forward, hold hands, and try to (simultaneously) pull each other up.

4. Trust Walk. Participants pair up into teams (partners) of two. One partner is blindfolded, the other is not. Players hold hands as the seeing partner leads the blindfolded partner on a walk through the woods. All seeing players should follow the counselor (leader). During the walk, the seeing player talks continually, telling the blindfolded partner to step over this and watch out for that. Before the walk, the counselor should map out the walking course to make sure that the trail is challenging enough, but not too dangerous for the age levels of the players. After the walk, reverse the roles—put the blindfold on the previously seeing partner; and now the partners walk again. After both partners have walked, hold a brief discussion to talk about what the players were thinking and feeling on the trust walk.

5. Peanut Butter. Number of Players: 6 to 100. Age of Players: 6 to 100. The playing area is a large grass field, completely empty of obstacles and dangerous objects. *Beginning version:* Divide the group into two teams with an equal number of players (if there is an extra player, let him help you as a guide). One team is the "Peanut!", the other team is the "Butter!". All players meet in the middle then close their eyes; eyes should remain closed during the entire game. (An alternative to eye-closing is blindfolds). The counselors mix the players so that the team members are not standing beside one another. At the counselor's announcement, the players (with eyes closed) take a few steps forward. The counselor blows a whistle, then the Peanut team-members shout "Peanut!", over and over again. Meanwhile, the Butter team-members yell "Butter!", and keep on yelling "Butter!". Each players yells, then listens for the sounds of his teammates. When he hears a teammate, he walks to him (eyes are still closed) and joins hands. "Peanut" team wins if they get all their "peanut" players to hold hands before all the "butter" players join together. During the entire game the counselors walk in circles around the throng. If an eyes-closed player begins to stray too far, then the counselor points him toward the hub of activity.
Intermediate version. Same game, except instead of Peanut! and Butter!, the teams are named (and shout out) "Giggle!" and "Jiggle!"
Advanced versions. Make three teams named Giggle!, Jiggle!, and Wiggle!. Or, make four teams who shout simultaneously: "Giggle! Jiggle! Wiggle! Squiggle!"; or shout "Futter! Butter! Nutter! Mutter!".

6. Rubber Blubber. A variation of Peanut Butter. Give each child in the large group 1 partner. The object of the game is to (blindfolded) find your partner. The only words you are allowed to say are either "rubber!" or "blubber!".

7. Giant Caterpillar. Ten kids (or 20 or 30 or 100) lie down on the grass on their backs, like 10 kids sleeping right beside each other in a bed. Shoulders must touch shoulders with no space in between. The 1st kid rolls over onto kid beside him, and keeps rolling over the bodies of the other kids until he gets to the end of the line. Then the 2nd kid rolls over; then the 3rd; and so on. Lots of grunting and groaning and "Oh no, here comes Big Bill!" adds fun to this game.

8. Sneaker Mountain. Number of Players: 6 to 1,000. Age of Players: 6 to adult. Play on grass. Everyone takes off their sneakers and mixes them into a mountainous pile. Divide the group into two teams; then stand on the starting line, about 100 yards from the pile. At the blow of the whistle, all the players rush to the mountain, search for the sneakers, and put them on. When a player gets his sneakers back on he dashes back to the starting line. The first team to get all their players back to the starting line with sneakers on, wins. *Variation 1*. Increase the fun by adding other events: after putting on the sneakers the player must crawl backwards on all fours, and so on. *Variation 2*. Instead of racing against each other, race against Time. The counselor uses a stopwatch to time how long it takes. Players help each other to find their sneakers.

9. Balloon Mashing. For this game you will need balloons, and string cut into pieces about 18 inches long. Give each player a piece of string and a balloon. Each player ties one end of the string around her ankle, then ties the other end of the string around the lip of the blown-up balloon. At the whistle, players run around and try to step on other person's balloons, while preventing their own balloon from being stepped on. Chaotic but fun!

10. Meeting of the Minds. This game is one of the quickest and most fun ways to get to know each other. It works best with a medium-sized group of anywhere between 6 and 24 kids. To play, stand together in a circle on the grass. The counselor asks a question (see the question list below), and the kids shout the answer. The object of the game is to get into groups as quickly as possible. Kids who shout the same answer must get into a group with one another. Kids who are the only one to answer must get in a group together consisting of all the kids whose answers are unique.

As soon as the groups are formed, the counselor asks the next question and then the groups must break up again into different groups. The faster you play, the funnier it is.

Question List for MEETING OF THE MINDS. 1) Your name? 2) City you live in? 3) Ever been to this place before? 4) Do you know anyone here? 5) What school grade are you in? 6) On a scale of 0 to 100, how much do you like school? 7) What is your favorite thing to do? 8) What's your second favorite thing to do? 9) Your third favorite thing to do? 10) How many sisters do you have? 11) How many brothers do you have? 12) What pets do you have? 13) Your favorite wild animal? 14) Your favorite dessert? 15) Your least favorite food? 16) What is your favorite book? 17) What is something you can do very well? 18) What is something new you would like to learn how to do? 19) Name something you want to do here. 20) Name another thing you want to do here.

11. Martian Sun Dance. Ask the group to form a large circle, with everyone holding on to one another around the shoulders. The leader should demonstrate the dance, then get back into the circle and join in. To dance, start with your feet together, touching each other. Take the to-the-right steps by stepping to the right with the right foot, then step (rightwards) with your left foot to touch your right. The steps are:
- 4 steps to your right, as you shout "Right! Right! Right! Right!"

- 4 steps to your left, as you shout "Left! Left! Left! Left!"
- 2 steps to the right, shouting "Right! Right!"
- 2 steps to the left, shouting "Left! Left!"
- 1 step to the right, "Right!", 1 step to the left, "Left!"
- 1 step to the right, "Right!", 1 step to the left, then shout "HEY!"
- 4 steps to the right (and begin the dance again)

Dance the dance either with everyone's arms around their neighbors' shoulders; or with all arms straight down at the sides and the all the shoulders pressed tightly against other shoulders. Everyone must be (physically) close to make this dance work.

Make up your own chants to match the rhythm of the steps.

Advanced version: instead of shouting "right" and "left", make up another word for this. For example: Right is "Bleep!" and left is "Bloop!".

Two–Minute Games

When time is short, or when a shy child is talking less than a giraffe with laryngitis—then often you can fill the time with fun, or open a rapport by playing two–minute games.

12. Slaphappy. For two players. The camper starts by placing his two hands out in front of him, palms up. The counselor (or second player) places his two hands, palms down, on top of the camper's hands. The object of the game: the slapper (the player who holds his hands underneath) tries to slap the hands of the slappee (the player with his hands on top). The player with his hands on top tries to pull his hands away before getting slapped.

After each attempt, players reset their hands in the original position, then play again. The players switch (slapper becomes slappee, and vice versa) whenever they want to.

13. Falling Buddies. Play this game on soft ground, or with a gymnastic mat behind you. Two counselors stand behind the camper. The camper stands straight up, then, keeping his body straight, falls backward. The camper must not try to break his fall by putting his foot behind him. The counselors catch the camper before he hits the ground.

14. Levitating Arms. The child, with his arms straight down at his sides, stands facing you. You grasp the child's wrists and hold them against his thighs, to prevent the wrists from moving. Tell the child to push both arms (not with all his might) so that the right arm tries to swing sideways to his right, and (simultaneously) the left arm tries to swing sideways to his left. The child will not be able to move the arms because you are holding them. Begin counting to 60, by "One mississippi ... two mississippi ... " and so on. When you get to 30, tell the child to push a *little* harder; a little harder than that at 40; harder at 50; and for 5 seconds (from the count of 55 to 60) to push as hard as he can. Now tell the child: "Stop pushing and relax your arms completely." When the child stops pushing, let go of his wrists. The child's arms will rise "by themselves", and feel like they're mysteriously floating.

15. Rock–Paper–Scissors. Before you start playing together with your kids you may need to choose who's it, choose who goes first, or pick team captains. Two games to begin your games are Rock–Paper–Scissors; and Dragon–Unicorn (See # 16). To play, each player places one hand behind his back, then shouts: "One, two, three … CLASH!". At the word "CLASH!", the players throw their hands in front of them. Players may throw:
- A Rock, made by a closed fist;
- A Paper, made by an open hand;
- A Scissors, made by placing the first two fingers into the shape of a "V".

The Rock defeats the Scissors (You say, "Rock breaks Scissors."): the player who threw the Rock gets one point. The Scissors defeats the paper ("Scissors cuts Paper."): the player who threw the Scissors gets one point. The Paper defeats the Rock ("Paper covers Rock."): the player who threw the Paper gets one point.

If both players throw the same item, then play the round over again. Play a best out of five set: the winner is the first player to get three points.

16. Dragon–Unicorn. The idea is exactly the same as Rock–Paper–Scissors (see # 15), but Dragon–Unicorn is slightly more complex. To make your Dragon, put out your open hand with your palm upward and all five digits showing, like a waiter waiting for a tip. Your Unicorn is one lone finger. Put out four fingers to make your Mermaid; three fingers for the Knight; two fingers for the Serpent. To play a round of Dragon–Unicorn, the players gather close together and place their hands behind their backs. Everyone counts together: "Three, two, one, CLASH!"—then each child throws out his hand. Each player may show any number of fingers he chooses: five fingers (Dragon); four fingers (Mermaid); three fingers (Knight); two fingers (Serpent); one finger (Unicorn).

With two players playing, the winner is the creature with the highest amount of fingers, EXCEPT: the Unicorn (who always loses to Mermaid, Knight, and Serpent) always defeats the Dragon. See the Mythology Tag chart on page 48, for a summary of who beats who.

When more than two players are playing, then after the kids have thrown their hands into the middle, take out all duplicate (and triplicate, and quadruplicate, etc.) creatures. (If ten children are playing and four kids throw Dragons, and two kids throw Knights, then take out all the Dragons and Knights.) After you take out the duplicates, compare hands of the children who remain.

If a Unicorn and Dragon appear in the same round with other creatures, then the Unicorn always wins. For example: if five kids are playing, and they throw out the five creatures (Dragon, Mermaid, Knight, Serpent, and Unicorn)—then the Unicorn wins. Why? Because the greedy Dragon first gobbles up the Mermaid, Knight, and Serpent—then the Unicorn and Dragon remain, and the Unicorn wins.

10

Ready Set GO!
How To Play Active Outdoor Games

Children need to play. Play creates instant friendship and enthusiasm. Active play and imaginative play are the ways in which children become friends with one another; learn about the world; strengthen their bodies; develop their minds and imaginations; and celebrate the pure joy of being alive. The child who learns to play well will learn the meaning of cooperation, joyousness, and intensity—everything she will need to accomplish great things throughout her life.

Here are three ways to get the games going that will give you and your group the most freedom and the most fun.

1. PRE-GAME BRIEFING. Explain to your group that in playing, the only things that matter are COOPERATION and FUN. Explain that playing to win is far less important than playing for the sheer joy of playing. The counselor should briefly share this idea with the kids, then make sure that he himself sets an excellent example.

2. LET THE KIDS CHOOSE WHAT TO PLAY. The counselor should give the kids some ideas, let the kids come up with their own ideas, then let the group vote for what games they want to play. Voting is completely democratic: the children have one vote apiece, and the counselor has one vote.

3. LET THE KIDS RESOLVE THEIR OWN PROBLEMS. Do you want to help to create self-reliant children? Then let kids make the rules, and let kids works things out when problems and conflicts arise. The counselor should intervene only:
   • When absolutely necessary, which means: intervene if a child is hurting himself or another person.
   • When the kids ask you. When children try but absolutely cannot agree, they may ask you to help work things out. Make a fair and objective decision; or suggest the compromise called a "do-over" where they re-play the disputed action, or start again.

The remainder of this section explains how to play the games that kids love best: active games in the open air.

Chart of 20 Great Active Games

Use this chart as a quick reference to find which game is right for your group, based on the number of players you have and their ages. To decipher the symbols: a "0" in the Equipment row means that no equipment is needed to play; "fb" means flagbelt; a "tc" means traffic cones; an "x" means other; "B" means ball; "D" means a plastic disk. An asterisk (*) after the game means this is an original game or variation never published before.

GAME	How Many	Equip-ment	Ages	Page
1. Spring Tag	6 to 30	0 or fb	all	46
2. Rock–Paper–Scissors Tag*	6 to 30	0 or fb	all	46
3. Four-Square	5	tc	all	46
4. Four-Square Squared*	6 or more	x	all	46
5. Capture the Flag	6 or more	x + fb	9 +	46
6. Scoring Keep-away*	6 or more	B	9 +	47
7. Banana Bandanna	4 to 24	x or fb	9+	47
8. Diaper Tag	6 or more	0	all	47
9. Mythology Tag*	10 to 30	x	9 +	48
10. Invisible Freeze Tag*	8 or more	B	9 +	49

How To Make Flagbelts

FLAGBELTS are standard equipment for many exciting outdoor active games. They can also be used as blindfolds; or as waistbands to identify which players are on which team. Make flagbelts out of a white bedsheet: a standard size sheet (92" x 72") will make more than 70 belts. Cut the sheet into strips 46" long by 2" wide. Larger-waisted players will need longer belts. Dye the strips into two bright colors, one for each team. Tie the strips around the player's waist by using a slip knot or a shoelace bow, so that the belt will come undone with a simple pull. Leave 10 to 12 inches of belt dangling from the player's back or side.

GAME	How Many	Equip-ment	Ages	Page
11. Counselor Tag	4 to 24	0	all	49
12. Glue Tag	6 to 30	0	all	49
13. Immunity Tag	6 or more	0	all	49
14. Flagbelt Promotion Tag*	20 to 24	fb + x	9 +	49
15. Three-Legged Tag	6 or more	x	9 +	50
16. Running Bases	3, 4, or 5	B	9 +	50
17. Spud	4 or more	B	all	51
18. Breakaway Ball	6 or more	B or D	all	51
19. Classic Dodge Ball	12 to 36	ball	all	52
20. Recycling Dodgeball*	12 to 36	ball	all	52

How To Play 20 Active Outdoor Games

1. Spring Tag. Team captains pick two teams, team A and team B. Each team selects a BASE (a place where they are safe from capture), and a JAIL to put prisoners in. Team A chases team B, and tries to capture them by grabbing them and shouting "7-8-9 you are mine!". Captured prisoners are brought to the base. Prisoners may be freed if a member of team B touches the JAIL and shouts "1-2-3 you are FREE!" without being tagged. After a while, or when one whole team is captured, let team B chase and team A run away.

Variation 1. A prisoner is captured only when you grab and pull out his flagbelt. For this version, during the game you will need one counselor whose job is to tie and re-tie all the flagbelts. To make the belts, see page 45. *Variation 2.* Play with three or more teams, each team has a base and a jail.

2. Rock–Paper–Scissors Tag. Played the same as Spring Tag, with one interesting exception. When player A tags (and thus captures) player B, both players stop to play a round of Rock–Paper–Scissors (RPS). If player A (the tagger) wins the round of RPS, then player B is officially captured. If player B (the taggee) wins the RPS round, then player B is free, and gets five seconds to run away.

3. Four-Square. The court is a square: each side is 24 feet long (adjust the length based on the age of the players). Mark the corners with 4 plastic traffic cones. The corners are the bases. To begin, four players (called runners) stand on the bases (1 player per base), and one player—called "IT"—stands inside a small circle in the middle of the square. Runners must stay along the baselines; the IT can run anywhere. The four runners try to run to another base, while IT tries to get to a base before a runner does. If IT reaches a base before a runner, then the runner left without a base becomes the new IT.

4. Four-Square Squared. Any number of kids can play Four-Square: just add on more bases and more squares. For example, for 8 players, have 2 squares with one common side: this gives you 6 bases, and two ITS standing in the middle of the squares. If you make 4 four-squares (in other words, make one huge square and divide it with two perpendicular lines in the middle), then 9 runners and 4 ITS can play. Use T-shirts to mark the bases when you run out of traffic cones.

5. Capture The Flag. The object of the game is to defend your own flag, and at the same time swoop into the opponent's territory, grab their flag, and run back without being tagged. The flag is a large, brightly-colored bandanna placed on the ground. Play on a soccer-sized field with a line (midline) that divides the field in half. Players are safe from capture while on their own side; when you cross the midline you may be captured if a player on the other team pulls out your flagbelt. Each team has a jail and its own flag, both located on its own half of the field. The jail may be placed anywhere in your territory, but there must be at least 10 yards between the jail and any of the boundary edges of the field. The flag may be placed anywhere, with the same 10-yard restriction. A team may not move its jail or its flag, once they have been situated.

Captains should make plans and strategies for leading the attacks and securing the defense. Start play by blowing a whistle. Players may run into the territory of the opposing team to try to steal the flag or free a prisoner. When a player is captured (by taking his flagbelt), then he is taken to the jail. If a teammate tags him when he is in jail, then he (and the tagger) can safely return to their territory. Only one person at a time may be freed from jail. The round ends when a player captures the opposing team's flag then returns safely (without getting captured) across the midline, then runs and touches his own flag. A player with an opponent's flag may be captured in his own territory.

6. Scoring Keep-away. Two captains divide the group into two teams. The object of the game is get the ball over your goal line. To do this, you may carry the ball over, or pass the ball over to a teammate. If you have the ball and a player tags you, you must give the ball to him, then give him 3 seconds to escape. During these 3 seconds he cannot advance forward, or pass the ball forward (but he can move or pass backwards). Unlike the game *breakaway ball* (see # 18 below), incomplete passes do NOT necessarily mean that the passing team loses possession of the ball. If the pass is incomplete, whoever gets to the ball first gets possession. However you cannot score a goal by an incomplete pass over the goal line: you have to run the ball over the goal, or complete a pass over the goal to score. Balls thrown over the goal incomplete, or balls thrown past the side boundary lines, automatically give possession of the ball to the other team. A goal scored is worth one point; after the goal the opposing team takes over the ball at mid field.

7. Banana Bandanna. Play on a grassy field to avoid scrapes; the field size can be as large as a basketball court. Mark the boundaries (goal lines and midline) with traffic cones or T-shirts. Captains pick two equal teams: each team contains 2 to 12 players. You need 1 yellow bandanna (or flagbelt) for each player. Place the bandannas on the midline of the field; weigh them done with stones if it is windy. The object of the game is to score a points. How? By picking up a bandanna, avoiding getting tagged, then carrying the bandanna across the goal line. To start, players line up on the goal lines at opposite ends of the field. When the whistle blows, all players dash for the bandannas on the midline. A player may pick up no more than one bandanna. You are safe from being tagged if you are on your half of the field. If you get tagged you must give your bandanna to the player who tagged you, and he may now try to cross the goal. Players must give the bandanna to the umpire after they have successfully crossed the opponent's goal. One point is given to a team each time a player crosses the goal. The round ends when the umpire is holding all the bandannas. Count the points, then start the next round.

8. Diaper Tag. Divide into 2 teams; one team chases the other. When a player is tagged she is frozen (must stand still). To get unfrozen: a teammate must crawl under the archway made by the frozen player's legs.

9. Mythology Tag. Select a person to be the Wizard to prepare, organize, and oversee the game. Select captains and divide players into two teams. With 10 kids there will be two teams of 5 players each. Each player is given one of the 5 kinds or creatures: the creatures are Dragon, Mermaid, Knight, Serpent, and Unicorn. If there are more than 5 players on the team, add creatures from the bottom up: the 6th player is another Unicorn, the 7th player is another Serpent, and so on. Each player knows what his own creature is, but the opposing team does not know. Each player receives a "pendant": a white card or piece of construction paper (sized 5" x 7"), folded in half around a piece of string. The string is tied into a necklace and hangs around the player's neck. Inside the card, in very small letters, the Wizard writes the name of the creature. Begin to play after every player is wearing a necklace-card pendant with a creature written inside. Play on a soccer-sized field, and mark out a base and a jail for each team.

Play starts or stops when the Wizard blows a whistle. The unique aspect about this game is that players on BOTH TEAMS may chase each other! When one player catches an opponent (or both catch each other), then the players show each other their cards. If both cards are the same creature, then neither player is captured. If both cards are different creatures, then one player will become the prisoner of the other. The player who captures an opponent must walk his prisoner to the jail. Prisoners may be freed if a player, without getting captured, gets to the jail and tags his teammate. The game ends when one team captures all the opposing players. Throughout the game, the Wizard may blow the whistle and stop the action: this brief stopping is called a "Time Bubble". The Wizard huddles with one team, then the other. During the huddle, the Wizard may exchange player's creature cards (*exchange*, not add other creatures) to confuse the opposing team, and to give different players the chance to be a more powerful creature. Make a big poster of the information below to tell you which creature captures which: note that the Dragon beats all creatures except the Unicorn.

Mythology Tag Battle Chart			
	Conquers	Has No Effect On	Is Defeated By
Dragon	Mermaid Knight Serpent	Dragon	Unicorn
Mermaid	Knight Serpent Unicorn	Mermaid	Dragon
Knight	Serpent Unicorn	Knight	Dragon Mermaid
Serpent	Unicorn	Serpent	Dragon Mermaid Knight
Unicorn	Dragon	Unicorn	Mermaid Knight Serpent

10. Invisible Freeze Tag. Pick two captains and two teams, and play on a soccer-sized field. Each team begins the game with one fist-sized rubber ball, but during the course of the game one team may possess both balls, and the other team none. One team runs away first, while the other team chases them. After one round (15 minutes), switch: the chasers run away, and the runners become chasers. The object of the game is to tag and "freeze" all the members of the other team before the round ends.

When player A tags player B, then player B is frozen: he must stand still on the spot where he was tagged. Player B can be freed ("unfrozen") if he is tagged by a teammate. Why the balls? ... A player who is carrying a ball cannot do three things: he cannot tag another player and freeze him; he cannot unfreeze a teammate; and he cannot be tagged (frozen). Balls must be carried in the hand, and not concealed. Of course, a player can throw his ball at any time. If he throws his ball out of bounds, the ball is given to the captain of the opposing team. As the game nears the end, it may happen that the last player on team B has a ball. In this case, this last player can be captured (tagged and frozen) ONLY by a player who is also carrying a ball. If two players on team B are the last two unfrozen players, and each one has a ball, then Team A must tag each team B player twice: the first tag makes him give up his ball, and the second tag captures him. At any time during the game, if a ball-carrying player is tagged simultaneously by TWO members of the opposing team, then he must give up his ball to the opposing captain.

11. Counselor Tag. Counselors play against the campers: counselors chase kids and try to tag and freeze them. Kids get unfrozen when they are tagged by other kids. One counselor has a whistle: when it blows, wherever you are, you change roles. If you were chasing someone, now you run away; if you were running, now you chase.

12. Glue Tag. Choose teams and play the same as in Spring tag. When a runner is tagged, however, he is not captured. He must place is hand on whatever body part that he was tagged on; and then he gets a head start of ten seconds to run away. Of course, he must continue to run while his hand is on the spot where he was tagged. When he is tagged for the *second* time, then he is captured and taken to the prison. After he is freed from prison, he can run normally again (until tagged the next time).

13. Immunity Tag. Play a tag game with any of the following variations. Immunity is temporary: players are given 10 seconds to rest, then 5 seconds to run away. A player or players are temporarily safe from being tagged when:
- The player hops on one foot
- Two players on the same team hug each other
- Two players on the same team lie on the ground and touch the bottoms of their feet or sneaker soles together
- Three players on the same team hold on to one another

14. Flagbelt Promotion Tag. Play on a soccer-sized field with two teams of 10 to 12 players per team. Have one hundred 3-by-5 cards and a marker handy. Give each player a flagbelt which he must tie around his waist in a slip knot (or shoelace bow), with at least 10 inches of belt dangling from the player's side. The two teams line up on their endlines (the opposing team's goal lines). The captains decide who goes first, and the teams take turns attacking and defending. Each round lasts ten minutes, or less if all the attacking players have either been captured or have crossed their goal line. In the following example, the Yellow team attacks, the Red team defends. Example: The whistle blows. The Yellow team and the Red team run to the middle of the field, toward each other. The Yellow team players are attacking, so they try to cross the goal line of the Red team. The Red team members defend their goal by trying to capture the Yellow team members: you capture a player by pulling off his flagbelt. If the Red team player captures a yellow player, then both players walk off the field together and report to the referee who is called the SCORER.

All players start out the game with the rank of "1". The highest rank is 12. There is only one way to gain in rank. When an attacking player crosses the opponent's goal line without getting his belt taken, he gains 1 point in rank. Now he is a "2". Gaining rank is important. A "2" ranked player, when he is playing defense, can capture two of the opponent's men: when he captures a man and takes him to the SCORER, he may return to the field and chase another opponent. A "3" ranked player can capture three men, then after capturing the third man he must leave the field until the next round. Rank means nothing to you when your team is on the offense: you still try to cross the goal line. Higher rank increases your defensive power.

A team wins when it is the first team to have any six of it's players achieve the rank of "12". Keep track of the ranks by giving out 3-by-5 cards with the rank numbers written on them. When a player advances a rank, he trades in his old rank card for the new one.

15. Three-Legged Tag. Make 2 teams; divide each team into partners of 2 players. Partners stand side-by-side, then tie their inside legs together with soft string. Frozen players may be unfrozen when tagged by a teammate.

16. Running Bases. Mark two bases, depending on the age of the players, anywhere from about 25 feet to 40 feet apart. Two fielders stand on the bases. One, two, or three runners start the game by standing on the bases. The runners try to run from one base to another. Each time they do that without getting tagged, they score one run. Runners keep track of their own runs. The fielders throw the ball back and forth, and try to tag the runners before they reach the base. Tagging a runner gives the runner one out. Fielders may go anywhere; runners must stay pretty much on the baseline, never more than about 6 feet on either side of the imaginary middle of the baseline. After a runner gets three outs, the runner becomes a fielder, and one of the fielders becomes a runner. When the runner starts out to run for a base, she may run back to the same base: there is never an obligation to run. Fielders may tempt the runners by throwing high pop-ups, or slow grounders. The highlight of the game is when a runner gets caught in the middle of a "run-down": when he is off the base, between the fielders.

Variation: More can play if you add more bases, and more fielders and runners. Or, more simply, just start more than one game. For 6 to 10 players start two separate games; for 11 to 15 players start three games; and so on.

17. Spud. Also called "Baby-in-the-air". Use a playground rubber kickball, or another ball that won't hurt when it hits you. The leader starts the game by giving a number to every player (including himself). Always use one more number that the total number of players: if there are 10 players, give out the numbers 1 through 11. The extra number (it can be any number from 1 through 11) is called the "ghost number". Whisper numbers into players' ears so that no one hears the numbers, and no one knows what the ghost number is. Write down the player's numbers on a card in case someone forgets. To play: the kids cluster together in a small circle around the "thrower", who yells out: "SPUD ... Number ... eight!" (the thrower can yell out any number between 1 and 11). Everybody, including the thrower, runs away form the ball as fast as they can—everybody except the person whose number was called. This person runs to the ball, and when he catches it he yells "STOP!". On hearing this "STOP!", all the runners must immediately freeze. The player with the ball may take three giant steps in any direction; then he throws the ball at any other player—usually the nearest. If the player had caught the ball before it hit the ground, then he is allowed to take five steps instead of three. If this player hits another player with the ball, then the hit player gets one letter of the word SPUD. If he misses, then he (the player who threw the ball) gets the letter. Letters are bad, and when you get S-P-U-D you are out of the game. Whoever gets the point becomes the thrower for the next round.

A funny thing happens when the "ghost number" is called. Everyone runs away, until someone realizes that it's the ghost number. Whoever is the first to realize this yells out "GHOST NUMBER!", then runs to the ball. When he gets it, he holds it out in front of him, and all the other players run to the ball to touch the ball. The last player who touches the ball gets a letter: S, P, U, or D.

Play continues again and again and again until you're too tired to play anymore.

18. Breakaway Ball. Play with a playground kickball, a football, or a plastic disk. A large area—a football field or soccer field—is needed. Captains pick two teams. Like American football, the object of the game is to pass the ball to a teammate beyond your goal line (but you cannot run the ball over the goal line). To begin, both teams gather around midfield. A counselor throws the ball straight up, and the team that catches it begins the game. Players without the ball may run anywhere. A player with the ball may immediately pass, or he may run as many as five steps backwards or sideways, but never forward. The pass can be forward, to the sides, or backward. After the player takes his five (or less) steps, he must either stand in one place, or pass the ball. If the pass is not caught (it hits the ground), then the ball is given to the other team on the spot where the ball hit the ground. If the ball is thrown over the goal line and not caught, then the opposing team is given the ball at midfield. If the defense intercepts the pass, they automatically become the offensive team. No body contact is allowed: defending players may block passes (swat them down), or wave their arms in front of a player who is going to pass. A scored goal is worth one point; after a goal is scored the opposing team gets possession of the ball at midfield.

19. Classic Dodge Ball. Two captains pick two teams (about 6 to 12 players per team), then decide which team will be the first to throw and which will dodge. The throwing team stand in a large circle; the dodgers get inside. Use a rubber playground kickball. The throwers throw the ball at the dodgers. Dodgers who are hit must leave the circle and cheer for their teammates who remain inside. When the last dodger remains, the throwers get ten throws to hit her. A thrower may pass the ball to a teammate, but this counts as one of the ten throws. If a thrower hits the last dodger, then the game begins again, but reversed: the throwing team is now the dodgers, and vice versa. If, within 10 throws, the throwers cannot hit the last dodger, then all the dodging team goes back into the circle and the game begins again. *Variation:* Play double dodgeball with two balls and a bigger circle.

20. Recycling Dodgeball. In this game the hit players do not sit out, they are recycled immediately back into the game. Pick 3 team captains who will divide your group (of 18 to 36) into 3 teams of 6 to 12 kids per team. Teams A and B should have the same number of players, and Team C should have the same number of players as Teams A and B *combined*. (In other words, Team C has twice as many players as Team A). Team A forms a circle, and Team B forms another circle: the circles are connected to resemble a pair of eyeglasses, or a figure-eight. Team C players go inside the circles: half the team C players go into the "A" circle, and half go into the "B" circle. If possible, the Team C captain should divide his team into two subteams of approximately even ability.

Use two balls. To play, Team A throws the ball at the Team C players inside circle A, while Team B throws the ball at the Team C players inside circle B. If a team A thrower hits a team C dodger, then the hit player changes circles: he goes from circle A to circle B. Every time a player is hit they go to the opposite circle. Multiple hits count: if the thrown ball hits more than one player, *all* the hit players move to the other circle. Thus, teams A and B are racing against each other: the winning team is the team that is the first team to knock all the players out of their circle.

Variation: Recycling Defense Dodgeball. Team C players may try to catch the ball that is thrown at them. If a team C player touches the ball but can't catch it, then that player is hit, and must go tho the other circle. If the team C player catches the ball, then he throws it back to the thrower. The thrower must carry the ball and run all around the circle, back to his original place, then hand the ball to the teammate on his left or right. (This slows up the progress of the whole team.) If a thrown ball touches one team C player then is caught (before it hits the ground) by another team C player, then it does not count as a catch OR a hit: just count it as a "do-over", and throw the ball again.

FIVE

BASIC COUNSELING SKILLS

11

How To Manage
The First Moments & The First Day

THE FIRST MOMENT that you meet the child is the most important moment of the entire summer.

Why? ... Because in that vital first moment, all children use their infallible intuition to ask these questions about you:

- Do you care about me?
- Are you on my side?
- Are we going to work and play together joyously, as equal partners and as best friends?

Throughout your friendship with the child, the way to say YES! to these most-important questions is to give children what they need. How? ... By being wholeheartedly sincere, by avoiding the blunders that most grown-ups make with kids, and by practicing the *Ten Things Caring Counselors Always Do.*

But when you first meet a child, remember these simple things: smile, be cheerful, look into the child's eyes, say the child's name. If it feels like the right thing to do, you may touch the child with a handshake or a friendly hug.

Now you are ready to move on to the next phase: start a conversation. Counselors, take note: this is the first step of a long and marvelous journey. The most important element of the camper and counselor partnership are the moments spent talking and listening to each other. Listening is caring. We must learn how to listen to children the way we listen to our best friends: with complete acceptance. Children will trust and respect any grown-up who takes time to listen in this way.

HOW TO START A CONVERSATION WITH A CHILD

What do you do to break the ice and start a conversation?

Ask the child a question.

Some ice-breaking questions are good, others are not-so-good. Not-so-good questions include questions that sting with sarcasm, questions that cause embarrassment, or questions that may remind the child of a fear—especially the fear of being away from home.

Not-So-Good Questions

• "Is that your face, or did somebody barf on your neck?"
• "Did you make any friends on the bus this morning?"
• "Are you glad to be here?"
• "You look skinny: don't your parents feed you?"
• "Do you miss your mom and dad?"
• "Didn't anybody tell you that you're not allowed to bring candy here?"
• "What do you have in that giant suitcase—a dead body?"
• "You don't know anybody here, do you?"
• "Hi, I'm Mike, your new counselor. Can I borrow a dollar?"

Good Questions

Asking the right kind of question shows that you are interested in the child's interests; you value her opinion; and you care enough to want to know more about the child. Good questions are questions that the child knows the answer to; questions about the child's hobbies or favorite things to do; or questions relating to the scenes around you here and now.

• "Is this your first time here?" (If the child says no, ask him about his previous experiences. If the child says yes, you can say, "Mine too," or "It's fun.")
• "How was the bus ride?" (If he threw up, ask if he needs a drink of water.)
• "Do you have a pet rabbit?" (If he's wearing an 'I Love Rabbits' T-shirt.)
• "Where are you from?"
• "Do you like playing army?" (If he's dressed in camouflage fatigues, a helmet, and a machine-gun water pistol.)
• "Are you two girls sisters?" (Said to two friends standing together.)
• "Can I help you carry your suitcase?"
• "Did you see anything interesting on the bus ride?" (If the child says no, you can say, "Well, there are lots of interesting things to see here.")

CONTINUING THE DIALOGUE: THE NOTE GAME

A quick and simple way to break the ice with shy and quiet children, or to continue the dialogue with a child you have just met, is to play the *Note Game*. The counselor begins by writing his name on a piece of paper, and writing a colon after the name, (e.g., MIKE:). Then the counselor writes a sentence or two after his name, and gives the paper to the child. The child writes back an answer. The game is played silently; no spoken words are exchanged. Kids really love this game! When more children arrive, have everyone exchanging notes to one another.

HOW TO LEARN ABOUT EACH CHILD

Erich Fromm has explained, in his important book *The Art Of Loving*, that to love something well we must deeply know and understand the person or the thing we love. If we are going to care about the child then it is essential that we learn as much as possible about children, and about this individual child we are working with.

Counselors can begin by finding out what things the child likes to do. The simplest way to do this is by asking the child. If your camp lasts for more than one week, you can make a poster, hang it on the wall, and each child can write down his or her favorite activities.

But sometimes, especially in the first days, children are shy and reluctant to speak. Another way to find out what the child likes to do, and other important things about the child, is to use the Camper Questionnaire (on the next page). Registered Readers (see Appendix B) may copy this questionnaire and give it to the children in their group.

REVIEW OF WHAT TO DO WHEN YOU FIRST MEET THE CHILD

- Give a **warm greeting** to each individual child: smile, look into the child's eyes, be cheerful, give the child a handshake or a hug.

- Talk to each child individually : start the conversation by asking a "good" question.

- Get to know each child by learning what the child likes to do. Learn about the child by listening to the child, and by using the *Camper Questionnaire*.

Camper Questionnaire

If you need more space to answer, use the other side of this page. You may write your name on the top, or, you do not have to write your name.

1. Write down three things that are boring to you.

2. Write down five things that you like to do.

3. What is your favorite thing to do?

4. Write down three new things that you would like to try.

5. What would you like your counselor to know about you?

6. Is there anything that you are afraid of or worried about at camp?

7. Write down three things that you want the kids in your cabin to know about you.

8. Write down three ways that your counselor can be the best counselor in the world.

HOW TO ORIENT THE WHOLE GROUP OF KIDS

By the time your entire group of children have arrived, you have already made great progress. You have warmly greeted each child, and talked briefly with each child, and let the child do 99% of the talking. Now is the time to remember that you have three goals for this first day: to make the children feel welcome and relaxed; to get to know each child; and to help the children to get to know one another.

Here (on the following page) is a chart that summarizes everything you need to do to accomplish these goals. But first, some practical advice about ...

HOW TO MANAGE NERVOUS AND INQUISITIVE PARENTS

All great things in life—and summer camp is one of the greatest things!—are ripe with paradoxes. The most surprising thing that you may discover during your counseling years is that the hardest children to work with are the homesick parents.

It's little Jerry's first time at camp, and maybe his first time away from home. Is Jerry nervous? A little. But Mom and Dad are a couple of basket cases. And if Mom and Dad hang around too long, then little Jerry is going to start getting homesick in a big big way. And other children, seeing Jerry's parents and recalling the comforts of home, may catch the highly contagious homesick bug. (see Chapter 19 for prevention).

Signs and symptoms of homesick parents include: 1) Hysterical weeping and wife dragging husband to the car; 2) Making and re-making the child's bed seven or eight times; 3) Asking questions about drugs or waterfront safety at camp; and 4) Offering you a large cash tip to take extra special care of little Jerry.

What every counselor needs is a Homesick Parent Management Plan. Voilà!

* *Be patient and polite with parents.* Answer all questions sincerely. If you don't know the answer, suggest that they ask the Head Counselor, or Camp Director. It is important to calm a parent's fears, and it is important not to let the parents interfere with your essential job of getting all the kids settled in. If this starts to happen, say politely: "Please excuse me. I have to get these children settled in. Can we talk a little bit later?" Then go to work (see chart next page) and let the parents hang out and watch.
* *Write it down.* When Jerry's mom reminds you Jerry gets sick if he eats peanut butter, you will remember until Ed's mother tells you he's allergic to chocolate. Jerry no peanuts, Ed no chocolate? Or vice versa? Write it down!
* *Plan ahead.* Your Camp Director should have a plan that says how much time moms & dads can spend with the child on the first day. When parents stay too long, the Head Counselor or Director should be the ones to break the news that it's time to go.
* *Tips about tips.* Parents may offer you an envelope to "take extra special care of Jerry." Find out your camp's policy about tips, then follow it. If your camp allows tips, and you take one, make sure that you ask the parent if the money is just for you, or if it is intended also for your co-counselor and junior staff. Send a thank-you note, too.

What To Do When All The Kids Arrive

When all the children in your group have arrived, be cheerful and friendly! Sit in a circle with the kids and do these things:

1	• Ask the children if they have any questions; then answer them.
2	• Show the kids the bathroom and the water fountain.
3	• If all the kids arrive at once, play Rock-Paper-Scissors to see who gets their first choice of beds.
4	• Collect medications and vitamins, if this has not already been done by the Nurse. Collect camper valuables and explain why.
5	• Give special individual attention to newcomers, or to children who look like they are afraid or unhappy. Make mental notes to talk later (as soon as possible), one-to-one, with these kids.
6	• Tell the kids about yourself. Tell what you like to do; what your hobbies & interests are; what you are looking forward to at camp. Say, in your own words: "My job is to help you to be safe, and to have fun here. If you have any questions, problems, or ideas, then you can talk to me at any time."
7	• Introduce kids to one another. Ask each child: Name? What do you like to do? What would you like to do at camp?
8	• Tell the kids the schedule or plan for the rest of the day today. Take a Tour of Camp. Give everyone a buddy, and buddy-up a first-time camper with a child who has been to camp before.
9	• During the tour, tell the kids all the basic information about the site and facilities. Include safety and emergency procedures.
10	• Play Getting Acquainted Games or Active Games with the kids
11	• Make two posters: Rules, & Games. Talk together to make a list of rules for your cabin group. Then help the kids to draw a large poster of all the games & activities the cabin group wants to do.
12	• Ask again for questions, then answer them. Continue with camp first day schedule, or play games together until the next meal.

12

When & How To Say "No!" To Children

Shy people, gentle people, quiet people—men and women alike—often have trouble saying "No!" to kids. They fear that if they say "No!", then the children will not like them. But of course, saying "No!", when "No!" needs to be said is one of the best things in the world that you can do for the child, and for your own survival. Pastore's 2nd Law mercilessly states:

> "If you can't say 'No!', you're dead meat."

Saying Yes is happy, fun and wonderful. But counselors need to understand that saying No to children, at the right times, is just as important for their health and happiness as saying Yes.

THREE IMPORTANT THINGS TO REMEMBER
WHEN YOU SAY "NO" OR "PLEASE STOP"

The Caring Counselor remembers three important things whenever he says "No" or "Please stop" to the child.

1. Say "No" or "Please stop" in a friendly and cheerful tone of voice.

2. Always explain WHY you are asking the child to stop, or WHY you are saying "No" to her request. Don't hurt feelings, but give the completely honest reason.

3. After you say "No", or "Please stop that", offer the child a fun alternative.
   For example:
   • "Joe, please don't play catch with the book I'm reading. It may wreck the book. Roll up a T-shirt and throw that around, or go get a ball from the sports shed." Or: "Joe, please stop. What else would you like to do?"
   • "Sharon, I'm sorry we can't have another dance tonight for evening activity. The rec hall is being used. Let's think of something else really fun that we can do."

WHEN TO SAY "NO!" TO CHILDREN

An impossible question because every moment in life is unique. However, there are three types of situations when "No!" is the best thing for counselors to say.

1. Say "No!" to Maintain the Health and Safety of Persons and Living Things.
Say "No!" when the child is doing something (or wants to do something) that endangers (or may endanger) his own health and safety, or the health and safety of others persons or living things.

2. Say "No!" When You Don't Want To Do Something. Children and adults have equal rights. When the adult appropriates all the rights (via the Do-it-or-else! Method), he becomes a tyrant. When the adult gives up all his rights (when he is afraid to say "No!"), then he becomes a slave. Working effectively with children demands complete sincerity: sincerity is the art of being yourself.

3. Say "No!" To Maintain the Freedom or the Rights of Others. Say "No!" whenever the child is doing something that violates the freedom or the rights of others.

Example 1: John, age 9, is carving his initials on a tree. First the counselor starts a friendly conversation, then he brings up the important subject.

Counselor: John, do you know what happens when you carve into a tree?
Child: No.
Counselor: The bark is the tree's skin. If you cut the bark, germs get into the tree, and the tree can get a disease then die.

If John keeps on carving, then the counselor should calmly say: "John, you can give me your knife, or you can stop carving the tree. What do you want to do?"
If the counselor has a good rapport with John, then John will stop when asked. If John continues carving, then the counselor could use the WE TECHNIQUE (see Chapter 19). Another idea would be to show John the importance of trees, by taking him on an outdoor camping trip. See Chapters 17 & 18 in this book; and also the short novel *Zen In The Art Of Child Maintenance.*

Example 2: Counselor Mike has been asked by his supervisor to plan a hike.

Camper: Mike, will you read me a story?
Counselor: I'd like to, but right now I have to plan tomorrow's hike. I'll read tomorrow night. Will you remind me? Here's the book. You can sit next to me and read while I work on the hike plans.

Example 3: It's 10 P.M., the lights are out in the cabin, and all the children are in bed. Arnold, age 10, starts making those classic cacophonous noises by blowing with his lips into the palm of his hand.

Arnold: RRRRRIPPPPP!
Counselor: Arnold, that's a great imitation, but please stop. The other kids are sleeping and I'm trying to get to sleep.

Will Arnold stop? Everything depends on whether or not the counselor has established a friendship and a close rapport with Arnold.

How To Teach Yourself To Say "No!"

1) Say "I want to think about that." Start with a small step: answer the child's outrageous request by saying that you want to think it over. Tell the child a specific time when you will give him the final answer.

2) Use Humor. What's the worst thing that could happen to you if you say "No!"? Imagine yourself as Prometheus, who dared to say "No!" to Zeus, king of the immortal gods. Zeus was so impressed with this act of courage he chained Prometheus to a rock. At dawn, a vulture ate Prometheus's liver; during the day the liver grew back; the next day and every day the vulture returned for his fresh chomped liver breakfast. The myth has a happy ending. After 600 years of agonizing defiance, Hercules chalks up another good deed, and Prometheus is at last unchained.

3) Say "No!" Creatively. One shy and creative counselor solved the problem ingeniously. He wore two T-shirts, a white T-shirt on top of a yellow one. The white T-shirt said, in small letters, "Sorry, but the answer is ... " The yellow T-shirt said, in huge letters, "NO!". Whenever he wanted to say "No!", he calmly lifted up the white T-shirt and pointed to the message underneath.

4) Practice. Stand in front of a mirror every morning and say "No!" to yourself, 20 to 100 times, using a variety of gestures, expressions, and tones of voice.

5) Treat the Child As If She or He Is Your Younger Sister or Brother. Big brothers and big sisters have no trouble saying "No!" to their younger siblings.

The breakthrough for the shy counselor comes when he begins to say "No!" to the kids, and suddenly he discovers—SURPRISE!—that the children like him and respect him just as much—or even more—than ever. First, establish a friendship and rapport with the child; then you can say "No" whenever No needs to be said.

13

How To Get The Kids To Sleep At Bedtime

Bedtime, depending on how the counselor handles it, is either a hell or a haven. In the deep dark of the night fears creep under the covers. Kids are afraid of the dark, afraid to go to sleep, afraid of the woods and the wild sounds of the summer nights. Many children, remembering mom, dad, and pet poodle poopsie, miss the warm, safe and familiar comforts of home. Most children, at night, feel isolated, cut off, disoriented, and hopelessly alone.

Why do Robot Counselors have so much trouble getting their kids to sleep? Because Robot Counselors fail to meet the child's essential needs. All children want bedtime to be happy and fun. At bedtime, each child needs one grown-up who will give him or her warm and reassuring personal attention.

Caring Counselors develop a ritual for putting the kids to bed. The children go to sleep because the counselor gives them the individual attention that they need. The essential idea to remember is:

All children need special individual attention at bedtime.

We will call this ritual the Bedtime Celebration, to emphasize that bedtime should be a time for quiet fun. Bedtime Celebration lasts approximately thirty-five minutes, and consists of three distinct phases.

- Phase I: Reading, Storytelling, or Talking With The Whole Group
- Phase II: Individual Talking With Each Child
- Phase III: Five-minute Quiet Talking For Everyone

The equipment needed for this activity is:

- A good book to read to the kids; and
- A watch with a timer that can count down and beep when you've set it for a specific amount of time.

Phase I: Reading, Storytelling, or Talking With The Whole Group

Phase I lasts approximately 15 minutes. When all the kids have climbed into bed, devoured the bedtime snack, brushed their teeth, and gone to the bathroom twice—then the counselor should give the kids a choice. The counselor asks: "Do you want me to read a story to you; or tell a story to you; or should we talk together about anything you want to talk about?" Of course, if the counselor has no stories to tell, then the choice is: read or talk together.

If the counselor is too tired to read, or too tired to read with the right amount of drama and animation, then he should guiltlessly tell the kids that he is too tired, and say "Tonight will be for talking." A camper may volunteer to read to the group, but this only works out if the camper is a good reader. The reading should be done with the lights out, under the light from a small fluorescent desk lamp. This adds a mysterious atmosphere to the reading, and allows the tired kids in the group to fall asleep during the story. After 15 minutes of reading, storytelling, or talking with the kids, proceed to ...

Phase II: Individual Talking With Each Child

Now the counselor goes to the bed of each child, and holds a very brief talk with one child at a time. Some Caring Counselors start by asking the child: "Do you want a handshake goodnight, a regular hug goodnight, a crushing hug, or the works (all three)?" After the handshake or hug, talk about something fun that happened today, or ask the child what he wants to do tomorrow, or just let the child do most of the talking while the you do all the listening. While the other kids are talking quietly to each other, the counselor goes from child to child for the private chats. Phase II takes less than 15 minutes for a group of eight kids.

Phase III: Five-minute Quiet Talking For Everyone.

Now, with the lights still out in the cabin, ask the kids to turn the flashlights off, then announce that they can talk quietly with one another for five more minutes. When there is one minute remaining out of the five minutes, announce that there is one minute left. The announcement does not have to be firm, it can be funny and lighthearted: "O.K., guys, talk fast, there is only one minute left for talking. In one minute, talking stops and sleep begins."

When the Caring Counselor has a good rapport with his campers, then Bedtime Celebration works every time. The children go right to sleep (or almost), have fun at night, and grow closer in friendship to the counselor and to the other kids.

Stories To Read Aloud Or Tell
& Books To Read Aloud

Here is a small sampling of the great stories and books that kids love. Ask the kids for their own suggestions, and add their list of best-loved books to ours. Read or tell these tales as playfully, animatedly, and enthusiastically as you can.

Stories To Read Aloud Or Tell

- Aesop's Fables *by Aesop*
- Andersen Fairy Tales *by Hans Christian Andersen*
- Arabian Nights Entertainments *edited by Andrew Lang*
- The Blue Fairy Book *by Andrew Lang.* Lang's superb Fairy Books come in a variety of colors.
- The Bold Dragoon And Other Ghostly Tales *by Washington Irving*
- Celtic Fairy Tales, and More Celtic Fairy Tales *by Joseph Jacobs*
- The Children's Odin: The Book Of Northern Myths *by Padraic Colum*
- The Children's Homer: The Adventures Of Odysseus *by Padraic Colum*
- Danish Fairy Tales *by Svendt Grundtvig*
- East O' The Sun, West O' The Moon *by George Webbe Dasent*
- English Fairy Tales *by Joseph Jacobs*
- The Golden Fleece & Heroes Who Lived Before Achilles *by Padraic Colum*
- Golden Treasury Of Children's Literature *by Louis Untermeyer, editor*
- Household Stories By The Brother's Grimm *by the Brothers Grimm*
- Indian Fairy Tales *by Joseph Jacobs*
- Just So Stories *by Rudyard Kipling*
- The King Of The Golden River *by John Ruskin*
- The 1,001 Nights: Tales Of Wonder And Magnificence *by Padraic Colum*
- Pepper and Salt *by Howard Pyle*
- Perrault Fairy Tales *by Charles Perrault and Gustave Doré*
- The Selfish Giant *by Oscar Wilde*
- Sherlock Holmes Stories *by A. Conan Doyle*
- Uncle Remus, His Songs And Sayings *by Joel Chandler Harris*
- A Wonder Book, and The Great Stone Face *by Nathaniel Hawthorne*
- World Tales *by Idries Shaw*
- Zlateh The Goat And Other Stories *by Isaac B. Singer*

BOOKS TO READ ALOUD

📖 At The Back Of The North Wind *by George Macdonald*
📖 The Borrowers *by Mary Norton*
📖 Charlotte's Web *by E.B. White*
📖 Green Mansions *by W.H. Hudson*
📖 Heidi *by Johanna Spyri*
📖 Huckleberry Finn; and Tom Sawyer *by Mark Twain*
📖 The Jungle Book *by Rudyard Kipling*
📖 King Solomon's Mines *by Rider Haggard*
📖 Lark's Magic *by Michael Pastore*
📖 The Lion, The Witch, And The Wardrobe *by C.S. Lewis* (see also the other fine books in this series)
📖 The Little Prince *by Antoine St. Exupery*
📖 Little Women *by Louisa May Alcott*
📖 Lord Of The Rings; and The Hobbit *by J.R. Tolkien*
📖 The Merry Adventures Of Robin Hood *by Howard Pyle*
📖 Otto Of The Silver Hand *by Howard Pyle*
📖 Peter Pan *by J.M. Barrie*
📖 The Adventures Of Pinocchio *by Carlo Collodi*
📖 The Princess And The Curdie *by George Macdonald*
📖 The Princess And The Goblin *by George Macdonald*
📖 Ring Of Willows *by Eric Barker*
📖 Robinson Crusoe *by Daniel Defoe*
📖 The Secret Garden *by Frances H. Burnett*
📖 The Story Of A Bad Boy *by Thomas Bailey Aldritch*
📖 The Story of The Champions of The Round Table *by Howard Pyle*
📖 The Story Of King Arthur And His Knights *by Howard Pyle*
📖 Stuart Little *by E.B. White*
📖 The Sword In The Stone; & The Once And Future King *by T.H. White*
📖 Treasure Island *by Robert Louis Stevenson*
📖 The Trumpet Of The Swan *by E.B. White*
📖 The Twenty-One Balloons *by William Pene du Bois*
📖 Two Little Savages *by Ernest J. Seton*
📖 Watership Down *by Richard Adams*
📖 The Wind In The Willows *by Kenneth Grahame*
📖 The Wonderful Wizard Of Oz *by Frank L. Baum*

SIX

THE COUNSELOR AS LEADER

14

How To Plan A Game or Activity

The most important aspect of the camp counselor's job is to take care of the needs of the children in his or her cabin group. The perfect counselor is the counselor who can keep the kids safe; be a good friend like a brother or sister to each child; and help the kids to be close friends with one another. Compared to these abilities, any other skills or knowledge that the counselor possesses are almost unimportant.

But the counselor is needed to do many different kinds of things at camp. One of these additional jobs is to plan and lead games and activities. Good activities add fun and adventure to the day. And good activities help to bring children who share this fun closer together as a team and as a family.

In this chapter we introduce you to the Game and Activity Planning Worksheet. Using this worksheet makes it easy to plan and organize any activity or game.

Two worksheets are offered here. One sample worksheet is filled out with an activity called Apache Relay. Another worksheet is blank so that you can fill in your own favorite activity. Registered Readers (see Appendix B) may make copies and enlarge this worksheet for their own use with kids at camp.

The worksheets contain all the important information about how to prepare for, lead, and play the activity or game. When you fill out these worksheets, write the instructions so simply and clearly that anyone could read it and lead the game, even if they've never heard of the game before.

Under "Skill Level", N = new player can play; I = intermediate ability needed; and A = advanced. Camper Min/Max asks for the minimum and maximum amount of children who can play. Note the important **Feedback Notes** section at the bottom. After you run the activity with kids, use this to record your notes about how to get the bugs out and make the activity better and better every time.

Camp Runarunamuckmuck
Game and Activity Planning Worksheet

Activity Name: Apache Relay	☑ **Outdoor** ☐ **Indoor**

For Ages: 9 10 11 12 13 14 all **Camper Min/Max:** all camp	**Safety Rules/Procedures:** See other side

Skill Level: N I A Other: all levels	**Duration: 30′ 60′** **Other:** 70′

HOW TO PLAY: An Apache Relay is relay race to complete a series of events. Two or more teams race; there are 10 players per team. Play on the ballfield. There are 10 stations (locations). At each station an event (skill, game, etc) is performed. After the event is completed the camper passes the baton to the next member of his team who performs an event at his station, then runs to the next station with the baton.

PREPARATION, EQUIPMENT & MATERIALS NEEDED: Set up 10 stations. [] matches [] candles [] cereal [] bowls [] spoons [] eggs [] rope [] balloons [] hammer & nails [] marshmallows [] 2 relay batons [] 2 buckets [] 2 tureens [] paper cups

STEP-BY-STEP DIRECTIONS TO LEAD THE ACTIVITY: Kids and staff work together to set up the ten stations. Instruct kids to do the event as fast as they can, then run to the base to get points. Events:
1) Cereal Eating: Bowl of dry cereal must be eaten without milk
2) Three-legged Race: Tie legs together & run the bases to home plate
3) Wheelbarrow Race: One person stands, while legs held by partner
4) Arms locked back-to-back: 2 kids lock arms race to home plate
5) DuckWalk: Hold own ankles with hands, walk from home to 1st base
6) Run: from first base to campfire site on ballfield
7) Firebuilding: Build a small fire
8) Roast a marshmallow: After fire is built, roast a marshmallow
9) Egg Carry: Carry egg on spoon; end of spoon must be in your mouth
10) Water Carry: Entire team plays this event. Fill a whole tureen with
    water carried in hands. Go from 1st to 2nd base.

FEEDBACK NOTES: Tell kids the marshmallow must be charred. Bring extra marshmallows for eating. Next time add water balloon events.

Camp Runarunamuckmuck
Game and Activity Planning Worksheet

Activity Name:	❑ Outdoor ❑ Indoor

For Ages: 9 10 11 12 13 14 all Camper Min/Max:	Safety Rules/Procedures:

Skill Level: N I A Other:	Duration: 30′ 60′ Other:

HOW TO PLAY:

PREPARATION, EQUIPMENT & MATERIALS NEEDED:

STEP-BY-STEP DIRECTIONS TO LEAD THE ACTIVITY:

FEEDBACK NOTES:

HOW TO TEACH A SKILL:
Eight Techniques & Tips For Terrific Teaching

Another responsibility of the counselor may be to teach one or more daily classes in a subject such as arts, nature, sports, or waterfront.

Teaching is an art that takes years of practice to learn and master. Great teachers know their subjects thoroughly, love their subjects passionately, and explain their subjects with patience, enthusiasm, and humor.

When you are teaching skills to children, remember the following ideas:

1. ALWAYS TEACH WITH A PLAN. Before the activity, make an outline that describes the most important ideas you want to convey. List, step by step, the things you will do during your activity. Each step of the plan should be challenging enough to be interesting, but not so difficult that it is discouraging.

For example: For an activity about teaching a child how tie a figure-8 knot, the plan might be:

1) Show the children a finished figure-8 knot.
2) Ask the children what a figure-8 knot can be used for
3) Give out the string.
4) Tell a joke or interesting story about string or knots.
5) Show the kids what the parts are: Standing End, Loop, etc.
6) Slowly, tie the first step in the figure-8 knot
7) Wait for the kids to get it right
8) Tie the next step in the figure-8 knot
9) Explain the similarities and differences to a square knot
10) Tie the last step in the figure-eight knot
11) Ask the children if they have any questions;
   then ask your prepared questions
12) Review by asking basic questions

2. LET CHILDREN PARTICIPATE BY DOING THINGS.
   Teaching by lecturing went out with the tyrannosaurs. The great key to interest is participation. Get kids actively involved in your lesson by filling the lesson with lots of things that kids can DO.

3) TEACH LIKE SOCRATES: ASK QUESTIONS, and LET CHILDREN MAKE UP THE QUESTIONS.

Another way to encourage participation is to ask the children questions about the activity. Before the activity, ANTICIPATE QUESTIONS. Think of at least 10 of the most interesting questions about your activity. If the children do not ask you these questions, then you can ask these key questions to the children.

Even better: let the kids make up the questions. Then let them work together in a group to try to figure out original, creative, and unique answers.

☆

4) USE POSITIVE SPEECH.

With every don't, say a do. For example, say:

"Joey, don't hold your hands on the bottom of the bat. (Do) Move your hands higher up on the bat handle."

☆

5) SIMPLIFY YOUR WORDS AND ACTIONS.

Even the most complex ideas in the world can be explained simply, directly, vividly, and clearly.

☆

6) ENJOY THE ACTIVITY and USE HUMOR.

The German writer Goethe said: "A man only learns about what he loves."

☆

7) END THE ACTIVITY WITH A SUMMARY and REVIEW.

Ask key questions to remind the children of the most important things they've learned.

☆

8) IMPROVE EACH LESSON.

After the lesson, make notes about what things need to be improved, and what things went well.

15

Create Togetherness:
How To Work Together
Like A Family and A Team

The skillful leader must understand how to create togetherness—not competition—within her group of children. How do you create togetherness? How do you transform your group of children into a cooperating team and a caring family?

People grow close to one another in a number of ways: by being completely honest and sincere; by working together; by playing and having fun together; and by talking and making decisions together.

Free and happy children will naturally make friends and get along harmoniously with each other. If you practice the *Ten Basic Principles of Child Maintenance,* and the *Ten Things Caring Counselors Always Do,* then this radiant feeling of togetherness will naturally come about. The passages below describe ways to encourage, intensify, and speed up the natural process. The following ideas will bring you and your children even closer together.

USE ACTIVITIES AND GOALS WHICH CREATE COOPERATION, NOT COMPETITION

Instead of having kids compete against each other, try these ideas:

• Set team goals, where everyone on the team loses together, or everyone on the team wins together; or
• Set teams goals, where everyone on the team competes against the counselors; or
• Race against Time.

Example 1. Using Race Against Time. The counselor wants the kids to clean the cabin.

❦ The Robot Counselor says: "We're going to have a clean-up contest. The kid who cleans the best gets 10 points; second best gets 9 points; and the sloppiest kid gets 0 points."

Obviously, this fosters cutthroat competition.

❧ The Caring Counselor creates cooperation. Her approach would be: "Kids, I'm setting my watch-timer to beep in 10 minutes. Let's see if we can work together and get the room cleaned up in less than 10 minutes. Get ready ... Go!"

In this way, as soon as Susan has finished cleaning her area, she runs over to help Jayne. Susan and Jayne work together; when they finish they help Alice, and so on.

Example 2: Use a Non-material Reward. The counselor wants the children to clean up the trash littered on the grass outside the dining hall.

❦ The Robot Counselor says: "The kid who picks up the most pieces of trash gets a candy bar!"

Can you envision the pandemonious frenzy of children pushing and shoving each other, fighting to grab a crumpled paper cup?

❧ The Caring Counselor takes the cooperative approach, and says: "If the whole bunch of you guys pick up more than 100 pieces of trash, then you can have 30 minutes extra free time. I'll help you. Ready? Three, two, one ... Go!"

CONVERT SOME COMPETITIVE ACTIVITIES INTO COOPERATIVE ACTIVITIES

A game of soccer or flagbelt touch football or capture-the-flag is competitive, but **played with the right attitude** it is worthwhile, because win or lose it's challenging, vigorous, and fun. *Some* competitive activities, however, should be converted to cooperative events.

Example 1: Obstacle Course.

❦ The Robot Counselor says: "I've set up this obstacle course in the woods. Let's see which of you guys are tough enough to make it through the whole course. Get going."

❧ The Caring Counselor says: "Here is our obstacle course—you guys did a great job building it. The goal is to get everyone through the course safely. If everyone makes it through before noon, we win; if even one person doesn't get through, we lose. Are there any questions?"

Example 2: World-Record Volleyball. Teams on both sides of the net work together and play against Doctor Gravity. The goal: prevent the ball from hitting the ground. Count how many times you hit the ball. Score 1 point for every hit; 2 points for every hit over the net. Kids can count aloud: ("One! ... Two! ... Three!") after every hit. After each round, try to beat your previous record.

MAKE TIME FOR THE KIDS TO TALK TOGETHER

From September through June, the daily schedule of the Average American child is more hectic than the rat-race supersonic tempo of a New York City executive. But to be healthy and genuinely happy, the child's life should move at a different pace: active but leisurely; energetic but without hurry or haste. Kids need time together to talk, to get to know each other, to build friendships. Make sure that your kids are not too busy to enjoy the simplest, most important things in life.

☺

TELL THE KIDS YOUR GOAL: TEAMLIKE COOPERATION, FAMILY TOGETHERNESS

At your first or second daily meeting, tell the kids that you are trying to bring about a group that works together like a team and helps one another like a caring family. Ask the children for suggestions about how to do this.

At future meetings, ask the kids to tell you and the group about instances they've seen or experienced where one child did something friendly or helpful for another. Children should be encouraged to report the helping and caring behavior of other children, and not to report their own altruistic deeds.

☺

TEACH BY EXAMPLE

Teaching by example is not the best way to teach: it is the only way. The way your children treat each other will exactly mirror the way you treat your children. We teach cooperation by cooperating. We create love by giving love.

16

How To Lead Open Meetings

The Caring Counselor knows that the great secret of working with children is to establish a warm friendship with each child. To maintain this friendship she will do many things: play with the children and have fun together with the children; share nature; treat the children as equal partners; and always be thoroughly sincere.

All these activities are essential for good relationships between grown-ups and kids. And the most important activity of all is this: the caring counselor will make time each day to have a one-to-one conversation with each child.

In addition to working one-to-one with the child, the counselor must work effectively with groups of children. One essential way to build a close family out of the group is to lead open meetings. Open meetings are a spontaneous and creative activity where children can talk freely, share ideas, and make decisions about issues that interest and affect them.

THE IMPORTANCE OF OPEN MEETINGS

Children who are never allowed to think for themselves, and to make decisions for themselves, will turn into Robot Children and Robot Grown-ups. Children who are given practical problems to solve, and the chance to choose what they want to do and need to do, will soon become independent thinkers and self-reliant kids. When children have become self-reliant, they do not need ceaseless supervision by adults. Self-reliant children know what to do, or know how to think for themselves to figure it all out.

By the way, don't think that these meetings are only for older children: children as young as seven (and maybe younger) can and should participate.

The Structure Of The Meetings

The ideal government for your group of children can be epitomized by the phrase, "Yours, Mine, and Ours." The Caring Counselor tells his kids:
"Some of the decisions will be all mine; some of the decisions will be all yours; and some of the decisions we will make together."
Decisions that are solely made by the counselor are decisions about the children's health and safety. Almost all other decisions, plans, and problems can be discussed at your open meetings.
The open meeting should take place every day, preferably at the same time each day. The meeting lasts from 5 to 30 minutes—longer, if the kids want to talk more. Each counselor in the group has one vote, and each child has one vote. Of course, one counselor vote is exactly equal to one child vote. Most issues will be decided by a majority ("most votes wins") rule; but in some cases the counselors and the children may want to imitate the Quakers: to decide anything, the vote must be unanimous.
The backbone of every meeting is the agenda: the list of things to be decided and discussed. We always start our meetings with the Joke-du-Jour (a volunteer tells a joke, riddle, anecdote, or a funny incident from real life). After the joke, proceed to the Counselor's agenda, then to the Children's Agenda.

The Counselor's Agenda

Agenda items that should appear at every meeting include:

1) Planning. Participation is the key to motivation. Let the kids take an active part in planning most of your activities. Kids can help you decide what you want to do; what preparations are needed; and who is going to do these preparations.

2) Praise and Encouragement. Children need praise and encouragement as much as flowers need water and sunshine. Praise the entire group for something genuinely praiseworthy. Publicly praise individual children for deeds well done, deeds that helped someone, or instances of creativity or ingenuity. If you get this working right, then the children will begin praising and encouraging one another. It is very important to keep mental or written notes to make sure that, by the end of each week, you've said at least one positive thing about each child.

3) Problem-Resolving. Problems are nothing more than opportunities in disguise. Problems are challenges to your creative powers, opportunities to learn self-reliance, and chances for your group to grow closer together like a family.

How To Work Together With Kids To Solve Group Problems

The counselor should be unafraid to use the meetings to bring up any *problems that involve the whole group.* Often, the simplest and best way to find an answer to a problem is to ask the children. This method is called "the WE Technique." The counselor begins the dialogue by saying:

"**We** have a problem. What are **we** going to do to solve it?"

Kids and counselors work together to discuss the problem, generate a number of possible solutions, debate the pros and cons of each solution, then vote on a course of action. As mentioned earlier, most issues will be decided by a majority rule ("most votes wins"); but in some cases the counselors and the children may want to imitate the Quakers: to decide anything, the vote must be unanimous.

Group problems should be discussed with the entire group. **Personal or interpersonal problems should be discussed privately, with only the individuals involved.** Discuss these kinds of problems one-to-one:

* Personal problems involving only one child.
  Examples: Karen's fear of spiders; or Mark's parents getting divorced.
* Interpersonal problems involving two children, or a small number of children.
  Example: Norton wants to beat up Billy.

The Children's Agenda:
How To Let Children Make Decisions At The Daily Meeting

The heart of the afternoon meeting is the Children's Agenda. Children raise and discuss—and whenever necessary, vote on—issues, problems, and ideas which are interesting and important to them. The counselor should participate by being completely open and candid; but the counselor should let the kids do 90% of the talking. After a few weeks of practice, the children should be allowed (on a volunteer basis) to run the meetings.

The counselors and children can share ideas, explore questions, solve problems, and vote on the best possible courses of action. Adults and children must learn how to work together as equal partners, sharing the freedom and sharing the responsibility.

SEVEN

CAMPING OUTDOORS WITH CHILDREN

17

Planning
The Overnight Camping Trip

THE POINT of it all is to celebrate the gift of life, and to love and to care for each other and all living things. To best enjoy these essential things, we need to make a careful plan that organizes the journey's 101 details. Smart preparation is the magic key. Then, when you get there, instead of worrying about who forgot the first aid kit and the hamburger buns, you and the kids can concentrate on living in the present moment and having fun.

Here is a simple sample plan for getting the trip going smoothly. Use this plan along with the *Nature Trip Planning Checklist* (pages 82-83), and one of the three equipment lists ins Appendix A. Change and improve these plans, forms and lists to meet your specific needs.

GENERAL PLAN FOR THE OVERNIGHT CAMPING TRIP

1. At rest hour (usually right after lunch): **PACK** your needed clothes and equipment, using one of our *equipment checklists,* or your own checklist. Help your group of kids to pack, making sure that they take everything necessary but not too much. Decide if each child will be completely self-sufficient and carry all his/her own equipment (then use List 1 in Appendix A), or if larger items (cooking pots, tents, etc.) will be shared (then use List 2).

2. Before you leave: **REVIEW the NATURE TRIP PLANNING CHECKLIST** (pages 82-83) and fill in all needed information. Count the kids and travel in buddy groups at all times. Leave a *Trip Emergency Information Sheet* (see Appendix A) with your supervisor.

3. **LEAVE IN THE LIGHT**. Depart for the overnight campsite early enough to get there when there's still plenty of light. You will need the light to set up your tents, and find lots of firewood.

4. **BRING ESSENTIALS**. Make sure that you bring these things:
   * A first aid kit and camper's medications.
   * A list of all persons who have life-threatening medical conditions, such as asthma or bee-sting allergies.
   * Enough drinkable water. By vehicle, take large plastic jugs of water to the campsite. Minimum amount: 1 gallon per day per person, plus more to cook.

5. **SET-UP** the site like this: 1) Choose places for the fire and tents; 2) Ask all the kids to gather firewood; 3) Start the fire for cooking; 4) Set up the tents as soon as the wood is gathered, while the sun is still up to light your work.

6. **HOLD A PRE-TRIP BRIEFING**. Meet with all the kids to:
   * Explain how to "go to the bathroom" without harming Mother Earth.
   * Review health and safety ideas for the trip, and the "Get Found!" packets.
   * Ask for questions and answer all the questions.

7. **FOOD & FIRE**. Show the children how to make a bearbag (see page 90) to keep the food from being attacked in the night by ravenous raccoons. Make certain that the fire is O-U-T OUT! OUT! OUT! before you go to sleep. In the morning, clean up: leave the campsite in better condition than when you arrived.

Preparing and Packing: What You Need To Bring Along

You can hike for a whole day wearing nothing but shorts, sneakers, a canteen, and a pocketful of gorp. But if you want to be self-sufficient, or be prepared for everything, then you need to carry a little more.

Use one of the three lists in Appendix A to create your own packing list. Our pre-packaged lists contain everything but the kitchen sink. For a short trip, no one would ever take all these things unless they had a covered wagon and a herd of camels. The value of the lists is that they are comprehensive: the lists will help you to remember many of the little things you might otherwise forget.

To help you to remember *all* the little odds and ends, use the *Nature Trip Planning Checklist* on pages 82-83, and the *Trip Emergency Information Form* in Appendix A. Zorba Press has kindly agreed to allow **Registered Readers** to photocopy and use these forms (see Appendix B).

NATURE TRIP PLANNING CHECKLIST   (page 1 of 2)

Date of Trip: Today's Date:

Name of Group:

Describe Trip:

From (Day & Time Leaving):
To (Day & Time Returning):

Departure Place, Destination, & Return Place:

BEFORE THE TRIP, DID YOU REMEMBER TO ....

FOOD & WATER

❑ Inform the Kitchen you need special food
❑ Prepare food that needs to be prepared in advance
❑ Clean and disinfect the canteens or water bottles
❑ Plan How & Where the group will get drinkable water along the way

MEDICAL

❑ Prepare and fill up first aid kit
❑ Get a list of children with special medication needs
❑ Get instructions about how to administer these medications

SUPERVISION & SAFETY

❑ Do you have at least 1 adult for every 8 kids? (more for younger kids)
❑ Leave *Trip Emergency Information Form* with supervisor
❑ Check weather report for upcoming bad conditions
❑ Hold a pre-trip briefing & discuss safety ❑ Give each child a buddy
   and a number. ❑ Explain the buddy system and the number system
❑ Review *GET FOUND!* packet with the kids
❑ Review *DO THESE THINGS IF YOU GET LOST* list with kids

NATURE TRIP PLANNING CHECKLIST   (page 2 of 2)

List Names & Ages of all Kids and all Staff Going Along:

Your Route (describe and sketch a map)

DID YOU REMEMBER TO ...

☐ Prepare a Packing List and ☐ Review it with each child
☐ Stretch major muscle groups before leaving
☐ check health of everyone before you leave

DOES EACH PERSON ON THE TRIP HAVE ...

☐ A GET FOUND! packet
☐ Dimes to call the main office ☐☐ office & ambulance phone number
☐ enough warm clothing
☐ protection from SUN, with ☐ sun screen and ☐ Brimmed cap

DID YOU BRING? ...

☐ An adult certified in first aid?   ☐ A First aid kit
☐ Special medications for kids   ☐ Maps
☐ Toilet paper   ☐ Small plastic spade
☐ Emergency Pack with: ☐ Knife ☐ Whistle ☐ Sunscreen lotion
   ☐ Flashlight ☐ Batteries ☐ Matches ☐ First Aid Manual

NOTES

☐ What is your plan to get medical help in case of an emergency?

PREVENTING AND PREPARING FOR MISSING CHILDREN

1. Leave a *Trip Emergency Information Sheet* (see Appendix A) with your supervisor. Tell at least two responsible people that you and your group are leaving for the hike or trip.

2. Have Adequate supervision. Best is a minimum of 1 adult to every 8 children, plus 1 extra adult for the whole group. For example, if there are 8 children, there should be two adults. For 9-16 children (quantity, not age) bring 3 adults. For 17-24 children, bring four adults. Children under 8 years old need more supervision: recommended is a ratio of 1 adult for every 6 children, plus one more.

3. Use the Buddy System and the Count-off System. Do a "Buddy check!" or a "Count off!" every 30 minutes or less.
• The Buddy System. Every child picks (or is assigned) one buddy, and you must stay with your buddy during the entire trip. When the leader shouts: "Buddy check!", take your buddy's hand, and raise your hands into the air. Then the leader counts to make sure all the buddy pairs are here.
• The Number Count-off System. Give each child a number which she must remember. If there are 20 kids in the group, then number the kids from 1 to 20. When the leader shouts, "Count off!", then each child yells out his or her number, in order (One! ... Two! ... Three! and so on). Ask the children why it is important not to call any other number except your own.

4. Be especially alert for younger children, less self-reliant children, slower children, or "adventuresome" children, who may be more prone to get lost.

5. Before you leave, discuss with the kids all aspects of Outdoor Safety. Give a "Get Found!" packet to each kid. Review these packets and the page: DO THIS IF YOU GET LOST. Ask for questions.

6. If a child does not want to go on the trip, do not force him. If a child is not acting well-behaved enough to go on the trip, do not take him.

7. Keep the hiking group together. If a hiker is going too far ahead, tell her to slow down. If a hiker is lagging too far behind, encourage him to speed up. When the leader blows the whistle, all kids should walk quickly and gather around the leader. When hiking, one adult should walk near the front of the line, and one adult should walk at the very end. If there is only one counselor on the hike, walk at the front of the line and keep the whole group very close together.

Counselors should explain the "In-sight" rule: Everyone must stay in sight of someone else. The last hiker in a line of hikers should never be more than ten feet behind the next-to-last hikers.

If you lose a camper on a trip, see LOST CAMPER in Chapter 19.

GET FOUND! PACKETS

Every child on a hiking or camping trip should receive a "Get Found! Packet". The leader has told the children to open the packet only if they get lost. The packet contains:

- The Instruction sheet: *Do These Things If You Get Lost* (below)
- Two dimes and a nickel for phone calls.
- Phone numbers of a main office, police, and the ambulance
- A sketched map of the trails & hiking/camping area (other side)

IMPORTANT! Make certain that the children know what to do if they get lost, even if they lose this packet!

DO THESE THINGS IF YOU GET LOST

1. STAY CALM. We know that you are looking for us. We are looking for you.

2. STAY IN ONE PLACE. Do not wander around.

3. DO NOT drink water that you find, and do not eat wild plants.

4. Read this whole page TWO TIMES. Look at the MAP on the back of this page. Then make a plan of what you are going to do.

5. If you have a whistle blow it 3 times every 5 minutes. If you do not have a whistle, shout "Hello! Hello! Hello!" every 5 minutes.

6. If you are ABSOLUTELY SURE that you can find your way back, then go to the trail and follow it. If you're not sure where to go, just **stay where you are.**

7. Follow these things to "civilization": a trail, a road, phone lines, or a brook or river (follow this downstream). Unless you're sure of where you are, Go downhill, not uphill.

8. Use rocks or sticks to leave a trail wherever you go.

9. IF it is dark, or approaching dark, then STOP and stay in one place. If you hear someone shouting your name, shout back.

10. If you get to a phone, call the main office at this number:
    If you need emergency help, call the ambulance at this number:
    There are coins for phone calls taped onto the back of this page.

STAY CALM!!! WE ARE LOOKING and WE WILL FIND YOU!!!

18

Basic Outdoor Living Skills

Children who learn how to do things become happy, self-reliant, and confident children. That is why children and Nature are the perfect blend: Nature is a playground filled with a thousand exciting things to see and do.

Practice these Basic Outdoor Living Skills and activities with your group of kids before you leave for your overnight camping trip.

* Firemaking in Four simple steps
* Ten Tips For Safe Campfires
* How To Cook Outdoors
* Backpacker's Notebook
* Questions and Answers About Safe Drinking Water

FIREMAKING IN FOUR SIMPLE STEPS

Step # 1: Gather Wood

All the wood you need, and more, should be ready before you light the first match. Gather wood and make three woodpiles: one pile for **tinder**; one pile for **kindling**; one pile for **fuel**.
* TINDER is small things that burn easily: tinder twigs are twigs with a thickness between the sizes of a matchstick and your little finger. Good tinder is dry grass; dry leaves; small twigs; thin bark that is dead; dry moss and lichen; dry pine needles; cones; dry grass stalks; and powdery bat droppings.
* KINDLING is dead twigs with a thickness between the sizes of your little finger and about 1" in diameter.
* FUEL is larger sticks and logs. Always use dead wood; never cut down live trees for fuel.

Step # 2: Prepare the Fire Site

DO NOT put the fire in a spot where the wind will blow smoke into your campsite. Clear a circle of ground at least ten feet in diameter; clear it right down to bare soil, rock, or sand. In the middle of the circle make a ring of rocks; if it's windy then dig a trench for your fire (diameter 18"; depth 6"), then place rocks around the inside border of the trench. If you plan to cook with the fire, situate some rocks so that you can place your grill (or pot or frying pan) on top of the rocks. Instead of rocks, you can use two large logs (first, wet the sides of the logs) placed on each side of the fire. These two logs should be about 7" apart at one end, and 4" apart at the opposite end.

Step # 3: Make An A-shaped Firestarter

In the middle of your rock-circle or firepit, place three thumb-thick pieces of kindling into the shape of the letter 'A'. The bottom of the 'A' should be placed so that it faces the wind. Inside the triangle of the 'A', place two handfuls of tinder.

Step # 4: Build A Tepee or Crisscross Frame With Kindling & Fuel

Two excellent styles to get and to keep a fire going are the Tepee Design, and the Crisscross Design. Whichever style you choose, arrange the thinner sticks first, then place the thicker sticks on top of the thinner ones.

The Tepee Design is made by laying sticks from an edge of a circle around the fire, into the middle—to form the shape of the frame of a tepee. Tepee fires are good for boiling water, or for sitting around to tell stories.

The Crisscross Design is made by laying two thick logs around the A-shapedfirestarter. Now place a number of sticks across these logs; then another layer—running in the opposite direction—on top of this layer, and so on. Fires need air, so don't cram your logs together so closely that the fire can't breathe. Crisscross fires are good for all-purpose cooking: frying, boiling, and grilling.

After your tepee or crisscross frame is built, light the fire at the bottom of the kindling, with a match or with a paper log (a tightly-rolled up piece of paper). Feed the fire with more kindling and fuel until it is large enough to meet your needs.

TEN TIPS FOR SAFE CAMPFIRES

Fire is magical, but fire can be very dangerous magic. Fire must be treated with the greatest amount of care, attention, and respect. No less a man than Henry David Thoreau, the world's most profound nature author, accidentally burned down a large section of the Concord woods. Before your trip, review these ideas about fire safety with your kids.

1. Never leave a fire alone: someone should be watching the fire at all times.

2. If it is too windy, then do not build a fire. If there is a significant wind, then build your fire in a pit.

3. Select a site for your fire that is at least 20 feet away from the tents.

4. Before you build the fire, clear the area. Clear a circle at least 10 feet in diameter. Make the circle free from all leaves and pine needles: clear everything away until you reach dirt, sand, or rock.

5. Lay a circle of rocks around the planned campfire. If there are no rocks, then dig a pit (18" in diameter and 6" deep), then build the fire inside the pit.

6. Never build a bonfire. Tonight's bonfire is tomorrow's forest fire.

7. Never throw paper into the fire: burning paper flies into the air. If you must burn paper, roll it into tightly-rolled paper logs.

8. Know your rocks: when heated, slate and limestone rocks will explode.

9. Always keep a bucket of water near the fire. If water is not available, use a bucket of sand or dirt.

10. When you are finished with the fire, PUT THE FIRE OUT!!! Start extinguishing the fire at least one hour before you leave. Break up the coals with a green stick (or a wet stick), then sprinkle water on the top. You must sprinkle the water because pouring the water may give you steam burns. Continue raking the coals and sprinkling the water. Turn over the larger coals and wet them. Cover the wet ashes with dirt; or bury them in your latrine. Unmake your firepit and restore the campsite to its original beautiful condition.

HOW TO COOK OUTDOORS

One of the unfortunate (or fortunate) facts about Outdoor Cooking is that you will undoubtedly be as bad (or as good) a cook in the wilderness as you are at home. Therefore, before the campout, have a number of experimental cookouts where you and the kids can practice making fires and improving your cooking skills. Have peanut butter and jelly sandwiches ready in the wings, in case the stewpot falls off the logs and the hamburgers burst into flames.

There are many ingenious ways to cook outdoors. Experts can cook in paper bags, on top of tin cans, or inside garbage can lids. Wilderness gourmets, armed with a thimbleful of yeast and a Dutch Oven, can bake scrumptious breads, cakes, and pies. But for me, after a long day on the trail, hiking 20 miles or biking 100, I am always too tired to do anything more than cook in the three simplest ways: boiling (or stewing) in a pot; frying and grilling; or cooking on a skewer. Whichever method you choose, you must begin by making a safe fire. Then:

- Let the flames burn down until you have a bed of glowing embers (also called glowing coals).
- COOK OVER THE GLOWING EMBERS, not on top of a blazing fire.

Food cooked over a campfire takes longer to cook than food cooked on your gas or electric stove. Essentially, however, boiling, stewing, and frying outdoors is just about the same as boiling, stewing, and frying at home.

BOILING or STEWING IN A POT. Aha! Notice that you need some way to support the cooking pot over the campfire. To solve this problem, you can:
A) Place rocks (or two green logs) around the embers, lay a grill on top of the rocks, then put the pot on top of the grill.
B) Place rocks (or two green logs) around the embers, and rest the pot on top of the rocks or the logs.
C) Suspend the pot over the embers, by building supports from tree branches.

FRYING or GRILLING. For grilling, start with support structure A, described above. Now simply lay the burgers right on the grill. For frying, structures A or B (above) will support the frying pan. A little soap rubbed onto the outside bottom of the frying pan will prevent it (the pan, not the food) from turning black.

SKEWERING. Start with a metal skewer and a towel to hold it; or use a green branch, shaved clean with a knife, about 4 feet long and ½ inch thick. Pierce the food, then hold the food over the flame, rotating the food so that it cooks evenly.

CLEANING UP. After the feast, boil a pot of water for hot chocolate and washing dishes. Clean up soon after dinner so the food does not harden on the cookware.

BACKPACKER'S NOTEBOOK:
Tips and Tricks For Living In The Woods

1. A BUNCH OF BANDANNAS. Bandannas are handy items. They can be used as bandages, hats, potholders, dust masks, wash rags, pouches, scarves, trail markers, rope, loincloths, and much more.

2. TENTS OUT OF TARPS. Plastic tarps can be rigged up in many ways to make quick shelters. Use a grommet maker to put grommets in strategic places. Instead of grommets, you can wrap a ball-shaped rock inside a side of the tarp, and tie it around with parachute cord. Do this a few times around the tarp edges, then you can tie the tarp to rocks or trees.

3. TYING THE TENT or TARP. Nature always provides. Camping on dirt ground, you can secure your tent by using tent pegs. Camping in rocky areas, you won't have any dirt to push tent pegs into, but you can weigh down your tent lines with large rocks.

4. WOODEN MATCHES can be made waterproof by dipping them into melted paraffin wax, or painting them with nail polish. Keep matches inside a plastic bag, and keep the plastic bag inside a waterproof container.

5. TENT FIRES. NEVER make any kind of fire inside your tent. Candle heat rises straight up. Even the heat from a small candle can burn a hole in the top of a tent.

6. BEARBAGS. Never leave food or garbage in or near your tent. Store food in a "bearbag": a large plastic bag tied onto a rope and hung high over the branch of a tree. Bearbags are necessary even in non-bear country, unless you enjoy late-night visits from skunks, mice, insects, stray dogs, and masked raccoons.

7. ACORN WHISTLE. For a very loud emergency whistle, take the cap of an acorn, hold it upside down between your thumbs, and blow across the top.

8. TRAVEL LIGHT. Take only the essentials and emergency supplies. Pack your backpack so that you can quickly get to the commonly-used items (sweater, water, map, etc.). Pack the heavier items on the top of the pack, and the lighter items on the bottom. The weight of your backpack and everything in it should be between 20% and 25% of your total body weight.

9. GOTTA GO. How do you "go to the bathroom" in the woods? First, be at least 200 feet away from (and downhill from) your campsite and all sources of water. For one-time visits, dig a hole with a metal or plastic spade, answer Nature's call, then cover the hole with dirt. If you're camping, build a latrine: a rectangular hole in the ground, 4 inches wide, 12 inches deep, and 2 feet long. Cover your droppings with dirt after each use. Fill the entire latrine with dirt after breaking camp.

10. BLISTERS can kill a camping trip. Blisters form from moist (usually sweaty) skin that rubs against the shoe. Prevent blisters by wearing the right shoes, and by keeping your feet clean and dry. Change your socks often, give your feet some air, and dust your feet with corn starch or foot powder.

11. CLEANING UP POTS & PANS. If you can get it, wet sand or small chunks of gravel scrubs better than the best scouring pad.

12. LOW-IMPACT CAMPING. Leave your campsite clean and in perfect condition. Pack out everything you brought in. Recycle recyclables; compost the garbage.

QUESTIONS AND ANSWERS ABOUT SAFE DRINKING WATER

How much drinking water do I need each day?
Adults who live outdoors require 3 to 5 quarts of water per day. Experiment on yourself and test, on a hot and active day, how much water you naturally want to drink. To measure the amount, carry an 8-ounce steel cup (you can clip it to your belt) and note how many cups you drink per day.

I've seen signs for "potable" water. What does that mean?
Potable means drinkable. NOT Potable means NOT drinkable.

How can you tell if it is safe to drink water from lakes and streams?
No one can tell without a laboratory test. Always assume that water from lakes and streams is NOT safe to drink. You can only drink this water if you purify it.

Can I use halazone or chlorine tablets to purify water?
NO. Halazone or other chlorine-containing disinfectants do NOT purify water adequately.

What are the safest ways to purify water for drinking?
• BACKPACKING WATER FILTERS. To filter out the infamous disease-producing organism called Giardia lamblia, the filter size must be .06 microns, or smaller. Filters must be cared for properly so that they do not collect bacteria and impurities, and become even more harmful than unfiltered water. Follow the directions that come with the filter.
• BOILING. Boil the water for 10 minutes, then cool it, then drink. For every 1,000 feet of altitude above sea level, boil the water an extra minute.

IMPORTANT NOTE: Iodine overdose can be fatal. Do not bring iodine tablets or iodine purification products with you when camping with a group of children.

Notes About Camping Outdoors With Kids

EIGHT

COUNSELING TIPS

19

50 Counseling Tips
From Aardvarks To Zippers

Here are various and sundry pieces of advice, some serious and some lighthearted, about more than fifty different topics of interest to camp counselors.

AARDVARKS. An endangered species in the New England states, aardvarks are nocturnal mammals with large ears, tube-like snouts, and powerful digging claws. The aardvark is not fierce, but when attacked it rolls on its back and uses its claws to defend itself. Seeing aardvarks is the first early warning signal of COUNSELOR BURNOUT.

AFFIRMATION CYCLE, The POSITIVE (PAC). The Positive Affirmation Cycle is the way that relationships between adults and children grow deeper and friendlier. Grown-ups who want to deepen the relationship must respect the child, play with the child, listen to the child, give the child freedom, and practice the 10 Basic Principles of Child Maintenance.

AGGRAVATION CYCLE, The MUTUAL (MAC). The Mutual Aggravation Cycle is the way that relationships between adults and children disintegrate. The child misbehaves, which prompts the grown-up to act mean and strict, which makes the child frustrated and behave worse, which makes the grown-up stricter and meaner, which makes the child behave worse—and so on and so on.

BANANAGRAM. A note, colored yellow and cut into a banana shape, sent from Caring Counselors to children who need cheering up or special attention.

BEDWETTING. In all cases of bedwetting the rule of rules is this: Do not humiliate the child. When the other children are outside playing, ask the bedwetter to help you to change the sheet. Many children are one-time bedwetters—that is normal. For repeating bedwetters, ask for advice from your nurse. You will probably be advised to restrict the bedwetter's fluid intake after dinner, and to wake the child at midnight, before you go to bed, and take him/her to the bathroom. Rubber sheets are available, to keep the mattress dry. Housekeeping for bedwetting is simple: blot the urine stain with paper towels or cloth towels, then wash with soapy water, then scrub with a disinfectant. If you don't have the rubber sheet, carry the mattress outside into the sun. Anti-humiliation hint: While the peed-on mattress is drying outside, the counselor should place his own mattress on the child's bed, so that the other kids don't know whose mattress is outside.

BLISTERS. Most feet blisters are caused by sweating skin rubbing against your sneaker. Hence, therefore, and thus: prevent blisters by keeping your feet dry. Use talcum powder or corn starch and change socks frequently.

BUDDY SYSTEM. A simple method used to prevent counselors from losing children. Every child picks (or is assigned) one buddy, and the buddies must stay together during the entire activity or trip. When the leader shouts: "Buddy check!", the buddies grab each other's hands, and raise the hands into the air. Then the leader counts to make sure all the buddy pairs are present. Can be used with the NUMBER COUNT-OFF SYSTEM.

BURNOUT, COUNSELOR. Symptoms include general tiredness; being irritable around kids (especially your own cabin group); and seeing aardvarks. After the second aardvark sighting, recuperate by going to bed the same time as the kids.

CAMPER PROD. An electrified metal rod that gives a mild but noticeable electric shock, designed for moving campers from one activity to another.

DEHYDRATION. Symptoms are dizziness and abdominal cramps. **Prevent** dehydration by drinking enough fluids during strenuous exercise. In a hot environment, drink a total of at least one quart of liquid each hour. Your total fluid intake per day should be between 3 to 5 quarts of fluids. Treat dehydration by giving fluids to the victim.

ELEPHANT MEMORY. A common mistake that counselors make with kids. When talking to children, counselors frequently use their elephant memories, and shout: "Today you pushed Arnold, yesterday you hit Kevin, a week ago you pulled Ann's hair, and two weeks ago you stole a cookie!" ... The effective way to help children is to *Take care of one situation at a time*. Forget about the child's past exploits. Respond to the *most recent* opportunity-problem with sincerity, calmness, and caring.

FIGHTS. HOW TO BREAK UP A FIGHT. When the aggressive child misbehaves, or gets into a fight, the only way to help him is by responding with warmth and calmness. NEVER let kids "fight it out"—that only leads to more hostility. Break up fights immediately. As you run up to the fighting children, yell in a loud and firm voice: "Stop!", or "That's enough!", or "Break it up!"—just to let the kids know that you're there, and that you are about to pull them apart. Step between the children and pull them apart. Separate the fighting kids as soon as possible—the fewer the blows that land, the better. Do your best to try not to let any punches or kicks strike you, or strike the fighters, as you are in the process of pulling the kids apart. If only one counselor is near the fighters, then he should grab the more aggressive fighter in the "baseball rhubarb hug" (a hug face-to-face, like a baseball player holding his teammate back), and gently push him back. After the fight, never force the fighters to apologize. Instead, let the kids calm down, then try to help the fighters to repair the broken relationship.

FIVE-MINUTE CALL. Before leaving a game that kids are having a great time at, give kids a 5-minute call. "We have to leave in 5 minutes!" the counselor shouts in a friendly voice. Also give a 1-minute call: "Only one minute left!". These calls gives the kids the chance to get ready, and to play as hard as they can play during the last moments.

FREEDOM, NOT LICENSE. This is the basic principle of human relations, formulated by A.S. Neill and practiced in his incomparable school, Summerhill. Concisely stated: "Children should be given freedom to do what they like, but no-one is allowed to hurt others, or to restrict another person's freedom." This abuse of freedom is called license.

GBUG (pronounced 'GEE-bug'). An acronym for "Go Before U Go". Before you leave for any trip with kids, take them to the bathroom, even if everyone swears that they do not have to go.

GOOD DEEDS, the TECHNIQUE OF. The Technique of Good Deeds is a technique for repairing broken relationships. If two children are not getting along with each other, then the counselor asks (but never forces) one of the children to do something friendly and helpful for the other child. The good deed makes both children feel happier: the child who received the good deed, and the child who performed it.

GORP (Good Old Raisins & Peanuts) is the classic snack food for hikers. Gorp is made of raisins and peanuts, and any optional ingredients you want to toss in.

HOLDING (PHYSICALLY RESTRAINING) THE CHILD. **When To Do It**. When the child has a tantrum, let him rant and rave. After a few minutes you can begin to talk to him soothingly. Holding (physically restraining) an angry child is a last resort: you should hold a child **only** when his behavior is a threat to himself or others. **How To Do It**. Use one of the two acceptable holds: the baseball rhubarb hug (see FIGHTS), or the front-facing wrists grasp (face the child and hold one wrist in each hand). Do your utmost to hold the child as gently as possible. Be calm. Look into the child's eyes and talk to the child in a soothing voice. Let go of the child as soon as possible. But if he continues to be a threat to his own or another child's safety, then hold him again.

HOMESICK CHILDREN. Homesickness is most common during the first few days at a new place. The child may begin by complaining about a tummy ache: even though you suspect homesickness, take the child to see the nurse. As soon as they occur, you should report all cases of homesickness to your supervisor: she or he probably has experience with this situation, and will be able to help you to help the child.

Prevent most cases of homesickness, and lessen the severity of other cases, by **immediately**—during the first moments and the first day—establishing a warm and friendly rapport with the child. TREAT homesick children by giving them special attention during the day, then talking with them before bedtime at night. Don't "smother" or "baby" the homesick child: give him lots of—but not too much—special attention during the day. When the child asks you the burning question: "When can I go home?", tell the child the honest answer: "That decision is not up to me; that decision is up to my boss." If the child asks to speak with your boss, then make an appointment so that the child can meet and talk with him or her. *Never* promise the child that he can go home; and *never* cut off all hope that he will be able to go home: both these extremes will aggravate the child's condition. With deep listening and special attention from the counselor, homesickness usually passes in a few days. Extreme cases may last for one week. The counselor can speed the recovery by finding activities that the child loves to do. When talking with the child, never deny his honest feelings (that he misses home); instead, try to emphasize the positive aspects—how much fun he will be having—at the place where he is now. Another good way to manage homesickness is to ask a big brother or sister, or another older child, to spend time with the homesick child.

If homesickness lasts more than two days, there may be a specific cause. Talk with the child and find out if he is afraid of the woods; if another child has threatened to beat him up; and so on. Discover the cause and treat it accordingly.

JOB WHEEL. A simple way to organize work that needs to be done. Cut cardboard into the shape of 2 circles, one larger than the other. Place the small circle onto the middle of the big one, and attach it with a paper fastener, so that it can be rotated. Draw slices (like a pizza) on both circles. On the large circle, write the jobs that need to be done. On the small circle, write the names of all kids and counselors. If you've done it right, then you rotate the inner circle so that one job matches up with one name. Each day, move the inner circle one place to the right, so that different persons get different jobs.

JOKE-IN-THE-BOX. Decorate a small cardboard box and place it in an easy-to-get-to place in the room. Beside the box, put pencils and 3-by-5 cards. Kids and visitors can write a joke on the card, then drop the card into the box. When anyone needs a laugh, just reach into the box and pull out a joke.

KNOTS IN SHOELACES, UNKNOTTING. Loosen knots by rubbing soap on the knot, then work the laces apart with a screwdriver or the file on your nailclippers.

LABELING KIDS. Never stick labels onto kids. If Joe hangs around you all the time, don't think or say: "Joe is a leech!". If Sam cries a lot, don't say: "Sam is a crybaby!". When you squeeze a person into one word, you fail to see the whole person. If Joe hangs around you a lot, don't slap a label on him: find the root of the problem, and solve it.

LABOR SAVING. In a group containing 2 counselors and 12 kids, the counselors should mentally divide the group to give better care and supervision. For supervising showers, teethbrushing, cleanups, and hikes in the woods, one counselor says to his co-worker: "I'll watch these 6 kids a little extra closely, and you watch the other 6." The next day, the counselors should switch sets of kids, so that they get to know all the children.

LIGHTNING STORM, CAUGHT IN A. Lightning strikes the earth more than 8,640,000 times per day. A bolt of lightning may contain a charge of up to 50 million volts. GET OUT OF WATER (lakes, streams, swimming pool, flooded fields, puddles) IMMEDIATELY!!! during a lightning storm, or if a storm is threatened. Lightning likes to strike a) metal things; and b) tall things. Therefore, during lightning storms you should stay away from metal things and tall things, and especially tall metal things. If you are in an open field or clearing, and you are the tallest object there—then get out of the field. If you can't get out, then lie down and curl your body into a ball like a scared centipede. (If possible, put something under you that will insulate you, such as a sleeping bag). Safe places are: under a shelter with a roof; inside a car (not a convertible); or inside a building. In the woods, scrunch down amid the small trees. Your tent will not protect you if you are in an open field; but a tent in the woods among not-too-tall trees is safe.

LITTLE MISS MUFFET SYNDROME (LMMS). Children who fear nature, spiders, living things, and living outdoors are children afflicted with the LMMS. Counselors who want to help children to overcome this fear may read and study the story *Sunrises And Starry Nights,* in ZEN IN THE ART OF CHILD MAINTENANCE.

LOST CAMPER. If you lose a child during a hike or a camping trip, **follow the procedures that your Camp Director has trained you to use.** If you don't have a procedure, then: 1. Stay calm. Keep the rest of the group calm. 2. Keep the rest of the group together at all times. 3. Check the obvious places: Did the child go to the latrine? Did he go to get water? Is he on the trail, lagging way behind? 4. If the child is not found within five minutes, then get the following information:• How many children are missing? • What are their names? • When was the missing child last seen? • Where was he last seen? • What does he look like? (Hair color, clothes, and so on) • Did he say where he was going? • Was he upset about something? 5. If another counselor is with you, one counselor should stay with the large group, and the other counselor should immediately report to the Camp Office in person or by phone. 6. If you are the only counselor with the group of kids, stay together and report to the Camp Office by phone or walkie-talkie. 7. Immediately after the child has been found, tell all searchers that the search is over.

LOVE-ENERGY is love made visible; love in the form of actions that you do with and for another human being. If I compassionately watch a child dragging his heavy footlocker to the cabin, then I am not giving the child love-energy; but when I help him to carry his luggage, I am giving love energy. Love-energy is love-in-action: having a baseball catch with the child; or listening to the child; or making the child laugh.

Love-energy is the great theme of the world's great teachers: Lao Tzu, Buddha, Jesus, Tolstoy, and Gandhi. All these men believed that one human being has the power to open and transform another human being by giving love-energy. Love-energy can be used to open the heart of persons, and to heal human relationships. A story about Abraham Lincoln illustrates this remarkable idea. Lincoln once explained to his staff that he believed a man should love his enemy, and with that love turn his enemy into a friend.

"That's nonsense!" a belligerent general shouted at Lincoln. "A man shouldn't *love* his enemy, he should *destroy* his enemy!"

Lincoln replied: "My dear general. I **do** destroy my enemy when I turn him into a friend."

MEALTIMES. Use the mealtimes to organize yourself, and to supervise children's basic health maintenance. Before meals, children should always wash their hands; after meals, always brush their teeth. During the meal, Caring Counselors look at their children to spot check for signs of physical or emotional bad health. Never force a child to eat, but if a child does not have much of an appetite, inform your camp nurse.

MISBEHAVIOR is action that violates the principle of 'Freedom, not License', i.e. any action that hurts another person, hurts another living thing, or restricts the freedom of another person. What causes children's misbehavior? Erich Fromm writes: "Destructiveness is the outcome of unlived lives." A.S. Neill, the founder of Summerhill school, says: "The difficult child is the child who is unhappy. He is at war with himself; and thus he is at war with the whole world." Of course, the Caring Counselor, knowing that unhappiness is the cause of misbehavior, treats the root of the misbehavior by giving the child freedom, sincerity, and unconditional love.

MOTHER'S MAXIM is the most important idea for keeping children safe. Mother's Maxim says: "Know where your children are, and who they are with, at all times."

NEEDS OF CHILDREN. In addition to the basic need for an environment that allows the child to be safe and healthy, all children have 6 basic needs. 1) The need for LOVE and FRIENDSHIP with grown-ups and other children. 2) The need to PLAY. 3) The need for FREEDOM to grow in their unique way. 4) The need to live and play in NATURE. 5) The need to do CREATIVE ACTIVITIES and the arts. 6) The need to learn and to learn HOW TO THINK: how to make decisions, how to solve problems.

NOTE GAME. A great way to deepen the friendship between the counselor and the child. The counselor begins by writing his name on a piece of paper, and writing a colon after the name, (e.g., MIKE:). Then the counselor writes a sentence or two after the name, and gives the paper to the child. The child writes back an answer. The game is played silently—no spoken words are exchanged.

NUMBER COUNT-OFF SYSTEM. A method used to prevent counselors from losing children. Give each child a number which he must remember. If there are 20 kids in the group, then number the kids from 1 to 20. When you shout, "Count off!", then each child yells out her number, in order (The kids shout "One! ... Two! ... Three!" and so on). Ask the kids why it is important for each child not to call any other number except his/her own. For younger kids, make it a game by giving each child a number *and* an animal: "One lion! ... Two tigers! ... Three bears!" etc. See also BUDDY SYSTEM.

ONE-MINUTE MEETINGS. Throughout the day, Caring Counselors have frequent one-minute meetings with the kids, which last from 10 seconds to 5 minutes. Gather the kids in a circle; ask how everyone is doing; tell a joke; praise the group for any caring, creative, or cooperative actions they have done; find out what the kids want to do now, then end with an energy cheer and a superhug.

OPPORTUNITY-PROBLEM. A situation where the counselor must respond to a misbehaving child. It is called an opportunity-problem because everything depends on the way the counselor responds. React with anger, threats, and punishment—and you hurt the child and antagonize the child. Respond to the situation with patience, humor, warmth, and sincerity—and you grow closer to the child, and help the child to become self-reliant.

PARTICIPATION, LACK OF. If a child does not want to play the game that the other children are playing, he should be allowed to sit quietly nearby and read, write, or draw. He is not allowed to wander away, because he needs to be supervised by an adult. Encourage participation, but never force participation.

RULES. Counselors and kids should work together to make the rules for the cabin group. Don't work on rules immediately: you want to show the kids that you are here to help them, not to dominate. Health and safety rules are made by the counselor alone: explain the reason behind each rule. All other rules can be made by the children and counselors working together. Children propose the rules, discuss them, debate why or why not the rule would be good, then vote on the rule. One all-purpose rule that the counselor should propose and pass is: "No one is allowed to hurt anyone or any living thing."

SECRET OF BEING WITH CHILDREN, THE. The secret of being with children is to establish and maintain a deep friendship and magical rapport with the child; and to give the child the gifts of freedom, love, and complete sincerity. Not merely during the moments when she "deserves it", but in *every* moment, even when she misbehaves. The way to create this deep friendship is to understand and practice the *Ten Basic Principles of Child Maintenance,* and the *Ten Things Caring Counselors Always Do.*

SCHMORP. Old gorp doesn't die, it just turns into SCHMORP: Stale Cold Hard Moldy Old Raisins & Peanuts.

SHY CHILDREN. Experiment to find a way to open a rapport with the shy child.

Children love puppets: give a hand puppet to the child, and keep one for yourself, then let the puppets talk to each other. Another way to communicate with shy children is to use the NOTE GAME. Another idea is to find a hobby or a special interest that you can share with the child. After the counselor befriends the child, the counselor can encourage the child to make friends with the other children.

SPRAINED ANKLE. To treat the sprain until medical help becomes available: 1) Elevate the ankle; 2) Immobilize it by tying a bandage around it in a figure-8 wrap; 3) For the first 24 hours apply ice; 4) After 48-72 hours apply heat. DO NOT walk on the ankle: reinjuries are very common. Seek a doctor to find out if anything is fractured.

STAINS. Terrified of their parents' wrath, many children become extremely upset when they get stains on their clothes. It is far easier to remove the stain than to change the parents' ludicrous attitude toward the clothing. For the best chance to get rid of stains, treat them immediately. The commonest child-related stains are:
•Ink from ballpoint pens: First, test the fabric to see if nailpolish remover will damage it; if not, remove the ink stain with the nailpolish remover.
•Blood stains: Rinse the stained garment with cold water, then apply a paste of meat tenderizer; then wash the garment.
•Ketchup: Scrape off the ketchup gob, blot the stain gently with a moist cloth, then wash the garment in an enzyme detergent.
•Juice stains, Chocolate stains, or Grass stains: Soak the piece of clothing in cold water for one hour; then rub soap or enzyme detergent onto the stain; then wash.

TANTRUMS. If a child loses control of himself, let him rant and rave to get the anger out of his system. Do not show emotion. Do not touch him. When possible, remove the target of anger (usually this is another child) from the angry child's sight. If the out-of-control child tries to hurt himself or others, then you must hold him without hurting him. As you hold him, talk to him in a soothing voice. Soothingly, ask simple questions. Tell the child that everything will be all right. Look into the child's eyes as you speak. Say things such as: "The fight is over ... Take is easy ... It will be all right ..." etc. The child will recover in a few minutes. What blows up, must calm down.

TEASING. Teasing hurts; and the counselor must stop the teasing as soon as it begins. If Joey teases Arnold, the counselor should talk with Joey. If the whole group tease Arnold, then the counselor should call a meeting and ask the kids how to help you to solve the problem. If the kids don't come up with the answer, then the counselor must be firm and clear: the teasing must stop immediately.

TICKS carrying Lyme disease are a serious problem in the Northeastern states. When walking in woods, wear long pants and a cap. After the hike, check the hikers' hair & body for ticks. Taking a shower immediately after the hike, and scrubbing your body, may wash away ticks that haven't had the chance to dig in. If you find a tick, see the nurse. If no nurse is available, don't pull the tick off: the head may remain in the skin. Smother the tick by covering it with petroleum jelly, then gently try to pull off the tick.

TONE OF VOICE. The *way* you say something is just as important as what you say. Whenever your tone of voice conveys anger—you hurt the child. Whenever your tone of voice conveys warmth, interest, and respect—you help the child.

TOUCHING. Touching is a natural way for healthy children to express affection. And touching is one of the best ways that the counselor can demonstrate her affection for the child. Of course, not all children will feel comfortable being touched by a counselor they have just met. **Use good judgment before you touch the child.** Has the child rushed to you and warmly hugged you? Then it's likely that she will be happy to receive a hug from you. If you're not sure if the child wants to be touched, then ask the child. Some non-intimidating ways to touch someone are: • Shake his hand • Hold hands while walking • Slap him five • Hug her • Exchange funny and elaborate handshakes • Walk with arms laced around each other's shoulders • Pat him on the back • Wrestle • Muss up his hair • Huddle together in a circle • Hold hands before a meal • Give a piggyback or shoulder ride.

Anyone who remains unconvinced of the meaning and value of touching should read Ashley Montagu's masterpiece on the subject, *Touching*. **Check with your camp director to find out what kind of touching he or she thinks is O.K.**

UNCONDITIONAL LOVE. One of the essential differences between the Robot Counselor and the Caring Counselor is the way they love and accept the child. The Robot Counselor, if he cares about the child at all, measures out his affection: he is nice to the child when the child is behaving, but he grows angry and unkind when the child misbehaves. The Caring Counselor loves and accepts the child in all moments. To love a child unconditionally means that you are on the child's side no matter what the child says or does. Children, with their remarkable sensitivity, always know which counselors love them unconditionally, and which counselors do not.

WE TECHNIQUE is a method for responding to children's misbehavior that works remarkably well because it asks the child or children help you to solve the problem. The counselor says "*We* have a problem; what can *we* do to solve it?"

ZERP FACTOR. The tendency of aggressive children—who desperately need caring human contact and affection—to not get that affection because their aggressive behavior drives children and adults away. The antidotes to the Zerp Factor are to give the child UNCONDITIONAL LOVE, and to care for the child according to the *Ten Basic Principles of Child Maintenance.*

ZIPPERS, GETTING THEM UNSTUCK. Rub a bar of soap over the stuck zipper, then pull, tug and jerk for all you're worth.

20

Summer Camp Jobs:
How To Find Them,
How To Get Them &
How To Keep Them

Every year more than 5.3 million children attend more than 8,500 American summer camps. There are approximately 350,000 staff persons needed to take care of these kids.

More than 350,000 job openings! You can get one of these jobs—and get one of the best ones—by studying and following the advice in this chapter.

HOW TO FIND THE JOBS

Here are the ten simplest and most effective ways to find out where the summer camp jobs are hiding.

1. Call the American Camping Association (ACA) at (317) 342-8456. Ask them for the phone numbers and addresses of their regional headquarters in the areas where you want to work. Then call these regional offices and ask about their listing of jobs. They will send you job application forms. You fill them out and they make them available to hundreds of fine camps. The American Camping Association is the nation's largest professional organization for the world of summer camping. They organize and sponsor numerous programs and events, and do everything possible to promote summer camping and ensure that camps offer the highest quality of service to all children.

   While you're on the line with ACA, ask them to send you a book catalog, and a copy of their *Summer Camp Employment Opportunities Booklet*. If you would rather write than call, the address is: ACA, 5000 State Road 67 North, Martinsville, IN 46151-7902.

2. Attend a national or regional American Camping Association event. There are scores of camping conferences, seminars, and presentations throughout the year. These events are not only educational and fun, they are **the best places** to meet the persons who can hire you. Your regional ACA office can supply you with a calendar of camping events.

3. Read *Camping Magazine,* published by the ACA. Camping jobs are listed in the classified advertisement section. Many issues contain a list of "job fairs" throughout the country.

4. You may want to take out an advertisement in the ACA's *Camping Magazine.* It is not cheap, but it reaches thousands of Camp Directors. You probably do not need to do this to get a good camping job unless you are applying for an administrative job such as Program Director, Head Counselor, Cook, and so on.

5. Read the want ads of the Sunday newspapers, especially the larger ones, in the region where you want to work.

6. Check with your university's student employment office. Camp Directors often send information to these offices. Also: many schools have "job fairs" where lots of camp representatives come and set up tables and fancy presentations to try to woo you to their camps.

7. Read Petersen's *Summer Employment Guide,* available at your local library.

8. Read ACA's *Guide To Accredited Camps.* This is meant for parents, but there is lots of useful information here. Use it to find out which camps would be places you might enjoy working at.

9. Most states have state camping associations. Ask at your library, then call your state association. Ask about job fairs, and ask for other information that they can send to you.

10. Ask children, parents, and other college students for ideas. This is one of the best ways, because you get an honest inside view of what the camp is really like.

HOW TO GET THE JOBS

To make a first impression that's good enough to get you to an interview:

• Start looking EARLY: December and January is the best time to begin. February through May is when most camp staff are hired. But if you haven't applied by June, don't give up: some camps still hire at this late time.
• Type the answers on the camp application. If you absolutely can't get to a typewriter, then print neatly.
• Answer ALL the questions on the application.
• Always include a résumé with the application.
• If you really want the job, include a personal letter. Write about yourself, your family, and your experience with children. Explain why you would like to work at camp. At the

top of your letter, mention all your current certifications relevant to camping. If you have any letters of recommendation, enclose them. Return the camp application (and other autobiographical materials) as soon as possible, preferably within one week (or less if you can!) after you receive it. This shows the Director that you care about getting the job.

STRATEGY FOR THE INTERVIEW

• Dress neatly.
• Arrive a few minutes early. Better to be 1 hour early than 1 minute late.
• Be prepared. Bring a list of questions that you want to ask about the camp (see list on page 106). Bring a list of points you want to make which describe you and your skills.
• Be positive. Smile often. Be cheerful. Be sincere, upbeat, and enthusiastic.
• Bring to the interview: letters of reference, certification cards, and an extra copy of your résumé. (Directors have tons of paperwork, they may have misplaced yours).
• Be ready to show that you have some kind of special interest in children or the child-care or teaching field. If your major is teaching, emphasize this. Also up-play (emphasize without exaggerating) your special skills (outdoor camping, sports, arts), and your hobbies and interests.
• Study and practice before the interview. See the list on page 107 for some of the questions that a camp director will probably ask you.
• Try to find out about the camp before the interview. Then you can explain how you can help. For example: "Mr. Pastore, I see you have a big archery program here. I taught archery all through high school ... "
• Do not be too quiet at the interview. If the interviewer feels that s/he could not get to know you during the interview, then s/he may not hire you.

HOW TO GREATLY INCREASE YOUR CHANCES OF GETTING THE JOB YOU WANT

You have a much greater chance of getting the job if you:

A. Have had some kind of work experience with children
B. Have any work experience that shows that you are RESPONSIBLE
C. Have any of the certifications listed below
D. Have taken one of the ACA courses or seminars mentioned above
E. Have read at least one important book (including this one!) about children or child management

All the people who I hire have one of the above qualifications. If you have two you are doing well. If you have three or more and you are a nice person then you would probably be hired by any sane Camp Director.

If you want to immensely increase your value as a candidate, then take this advice:

Get certified, get certified, get certified. Camp Directors need certified staff to meet stringent inspection requirements. Especially valuable are American Red Cross Lifeguard Training (LT); Water Safety Instructor (WSI); Red Cross Standard First Aid (SFA) and BLS CPR. Your local American Red Cross chapter has all the information, but it's cheaper and easier to take these courses at your university.

Camps offering archery need staff certified from one of the official Archery Instructor courses. There are also helpful certifications available in Outdoor Living Skills (OLS): ask your regional ACA office about this OLS training program.

Your Camp Director may be willing to pay for all or part of these training courses, if s/he thinks you will do a great job. If you have an interest in getting certified in any of these fields, mention it in your cover letter or at the interview.

HOW TO FIND OUT IF THE CAMP
IS THE RIGHT ONE FOR YOU

If you are reasonably intelligent, follow the above advice, and try your best and keep trying, then you can safely assume that you will find a job in the camping world. The important question is: How do you find out if this particular camp is a place where you will be happy? That is a very difficult question and possibly the only way to answer it is to spend a summer there. But it helps to find out all you can about the camp.

• Ask the Camp Director if the camp requires a personal interview before hiring. Think twice before working at a camp who would hire someone without meeting them.
• See the camp, if possible. But since that is not always possible, meet someone (Director, Assistant Director, Head Counselor) in the camp administration.
• Ask if the camp is accredited by the ACA. An accredited camp must meet the highest possible standards in Health, Program, Personnel, and all aspects of camping. But remember that there are many fine camps that are not accredited.
• Ask how long the camp has existed, and how long the director has been with the camp.
• Ask if there have been any fatalities or serious accidents at the camp in the last 3 years.
• Ask how many children attend, what their ages are, and what is the ratio of staff to campers. One staff person for every 8 campers is O.K.; but better is one staff person for every 6 campers, or even lower.
• Find out exactly what your job will be. Ask for a job description—but remember that job descriptions are "stuffy" and rarely tell you what it's really like. Get a daily schedule, and ask what the person who takes the job you are applying for will be doing at every moment of the typical camp day.
• Take home a copy of: ▤ a camp brochure ▤ the personnel policies ▤ a camp staff manual ▤ a daily schedule ▤ a job description
• When you get home after the interview, ask yourself if you liked the person who interviewed you. If no, then think two or three times before accepting the job.
• Be extremely cautious if the person who interviews you describes the camp as a

complete paradise. Many camps are great, but no camp is a paradise. Many of the complete paradises I have been told about are a lot closer to the other place. **Camp is a great place to be but the work is extremely difficult.** Anyone in the business who tells you differently is either a liar or a fool.

• The best advice is: **Go to as many interviews as you can.** This will sharpen your skills, and allow you to compare camps.

QUESTIONS YOU MAY BE ASKED
AT A SUMMER CAMP JOB INTERVIEW

Practice by answering these questions with a friend. Another excellent way to practice is to write down your answers.

1. I have just explained the camp rules and personnel policies. Do you think you will be able to abide by them and be happy?
2. Every staff member has two positions: counselor and activity leader. How will you manage that?
3. Why do you want to work for long hours and low pay at camp, instead of a higher paying job somewhere else?
4. Tell me about yourself. What are your goals? What do you like to do?
5. If you are hired, what do you think this summer will be like?
6. When should a counselor use physical force with a child?
7. What would you do if the you ask the child to come to the dining hall with you, and the child absolutely refuses?
8. Describe the perfect camp counselor.
9. Have you worked at camp before? Tell me about it. What were the things you liked and didn't like about the camp?
10. Have you worked with children in other situations besides camp?
11. Have you been to camp before as a counselor or camper? Tell me about it. Describe the best and the worst things about the camp.
12. What are your hobbies or special interests?
13. If you had one year off with enough money to do whatever you wanted to do, how would you spend the year?
14. Many staff undergo "Counselor Burnout" during the 4th week of camp. What will you do to prevent that?
15. Tell me what you imagine that the counselor will be doing all day.
16. Tell me some things that you know about children.
17. What age children would you like to work with? Why that age?
18. There are many rules and not much privacy at camp. How will you cope?
19. Camp is a simple life without luxury or even electricity. Comment on this.
20. Describe some ways that you would help to make the camp into a community of people who care.

How To Keep The Job When You Get It

Let us assume that you definitely want to:

- Keep your job throughout the summer, and avoid getting the proverbial ax;
- Earn the option to return to work at the same camp the next summer, possibly with a salary increase or a promotion or both; and
- Leave with a good or an outstanding reference that will help you in the quest to find a permanent, full-time, higher-paying job in the highly-competitive outside world.

To do this you need to take your camp job seriously and give it your best efforts. Let's figure out precisely how by using empathy. Step in to the mind and heart of your employer, the Camp Director. What does a Camp Director want and need most? ... Caring Counselors. Caring Counselors possess these four essential qualities:

1) **Responsibility**. Be where you are supposed to be when you are supposed to be there. Understand the "why" behind the camp rules and policies, and abide by these rules and policies.

2) **Good judgment**. Think about safety at all times. PREVENT accidents from happening by having the foresight to say to children the word "NO".

3) **Enthusiasm and a positive attitude**. This is so important!!! Give the small world around you all your happy enthusiasm and positive energy.

4) **Caring**. Care about the children, and care about the job you have been hired to do. Learn how to put the needs of others before your own personal and selfish needs. Real caring is more than kind feelings. Real caring is ACTION: things you DO for other persons and for the camp community.

Coda

Summer camp counseling is hard work. Hard work, but work is that deeply fulfilling and immeasurably meaningful. As a Caring Counselor, you are a very important human being. By caring, you have the power to help a child, to teach a child, to listen to a child, to share happy moments with a child, to transform a child's life.

Summer camping helps children to grow as happy, creative, and loving human beings. The caring you give makes all the difference.

Appendixes & Serendipity

Appendix A: Useful Camping Trip Forms 📃

📃 Trip Emergency Information Form   111
📃 Equipment List 1 for Overnight Hikes   112
📃 Equipment List 2 for Overnight Hikes   113
📃 Equipment List 3 for Day Hikes   114

Appendix B: The Zorba Press Registered Reader Program   115

About the Author   116

Great Books from Zorba Press   117

Order Form For Zorba Press Books   118

TRIP EMERGENCY INFORMATION FORM

Name of Group:	Date(s) of Trip:

Number of kids: Number of Staff:

Names and Ages of Kids:

Names and Ages of Staff:

Total Number of Persons on the Trip:

Departure Day, Time, Place:	Destination(s):

Estimated Return Day, Time, and Place:

Route (describe and sketch a map on other side):

❏ Does any child or adult on the trip have special medical conditions or needs? If yes, give names (use other side) and describe conditions/needs.

SPECIAL NOTES

Overnight Camping Trip Equipment List 1: Each Camper is Self-Sufficient	
Part A: Carried by each camper (◇ means optional)	
Clothing & Bedding	**Health & Survival Kit:**

❑ backpack or knapsack
 ❑ sleeping bag or blankets
 ❑ boots, walking shoes, or sneakers
 ❑ sweatshirt or light sweater
 ❑ jacket or wool sweater
 ❑ sneakers or soft "in-camp" shoes
 ❑ socks, 2 or 3 extra pairs
 ❑ brimmed cap (sun protection)
 ❑ long pants ❑ sweatpants
 ❑ extra shirt, t-shirt, underwear
 	
 ❑ sandals ◇
 ❑ poncho or rain jacket ◇
 ❑ wool cap (brightly colored) ◇
 ❑ bathing suit ◇
 ❑ long underwear bottoms ◇
 	
 Personal
 	
 ❑ wwck: watch, wallet, cash, keys
 ❑ glasses case, crushproof
 ❑ 2 bandannas ❑ plastic bags, clear
 ❑ 4 octopus straps
 ❑ notepad ❑ books ❑ pen or pencil
 ❑ needles and thread
 ❑ flute, guitar, or baby grand piano ◇
	❑ toothbrush & holder ❑ toothpaste
	 ❑ foot care kit: (❑ cornstarch or
	 foot powder ❑ moleskin pads
	     ❑ adhesive bandages)
	 ❑ swiss army knife or pocket knife
	 ❑ first aid kit: (❑ adhesive tape
	   ❑ gauze bandage ❑ bandages (12)
	   ❑ soap ❑ petroleum jelly
	     ❑ tweezers ❑ first aid book)
	 ❑ sunscreen lotion
	 ❑ ❑ maps and compass
	 ❑ 50 feet of parachute cord
	 ❑ $ 1.00 worth of change
	 ❑ emergency phone numbers
	 ❑ flashlight ❑ spare batteries & bulb
	 ❑ wood matches (waterproofed, in a
	   waterproof container)
	 ❑ pocket mirror for signaling
	 ❑ candle ❑ fishhooks and nylon line
	 ❑ plastic spade ❑ toilet paper
	
	 Food and Water
	
	 ❑ 2 canteens or plastic water bottles
	 ❑ gorp or hi-energy snack food

Part B (Carried by each camper)	
❑ tent or tarp ❑ tent pegs, poles, lines ❑ thick plastic sheet (flysheet) ❑ foam pad or air mattress ◇ ❑ groundcloth for sleeping on ◇ ❑ garbage bag, small ❑ enough food for the trip ❑ emergency survival food ❑ backpacking water filter ◇	❑ cooking pot, small ❑ frying pan, small ◇ ❑ can opener ◇ ❑ steel drinking cup ❑ spoon ❑ dishrag ❑ scrub brush ❑ dish soap (sm. bottle, biodegradable)

Overnight Camping Trip Equipment List 2: Larger Items Are Shared
Part A: Carried by each camper (◇ means optional)

Clothing & Bedding	Health & Survival Kit:
☐ backpack or knapsack	☐ toothbrush & holder ☐ toothpaste
☐ sleeping bag or blankets	☐ foot care kit: (☐ cornstarch or
☐ boots, walking shoes, or sneakers	foot powder ☐ moleskin pads
☐ sweatshirt or light sweater	☐ bandages)
☐ jacket or wool sweater	☐ swiss army knife or pocket knife
☐ sneakers or soft "in-camp" shoes	☐ first aid kit: (☐ adhesive tape
☐ socks, 2 or 3 extra pairs	☐ gauze bandage ☐ bandages (12)
☐ brimmed cap (sun protection)	☐ soap ☐ petroleum jelly
☐ long pants ☐ sweatpants	☐ tweezers ☐ first aid book)
☐ extra shirt, T-shirt, underwear	☐ sunscreen lotion
☐ sandals ◇	☐ ☐ maps and compass
☐ poncho or rain jacket ◇	☐ 50 feet of parachute cord
☐ wool cap (brightly colored) ◇	☐ $ 1.00 worth of change
☐ bathing suit ◇	☐ emergency phone numbers
☐ long underwear bottoms ◇	☐ flashlight ☐ spare batteries & bulb
	☐ wood matches (waterproofed, in a
Personal	waterproof container)
	☐ pocket mirror for signaling
☐ wwck: watch, wallet, cash, keys	☐ candle ☐ fishhooks and nylon line
☐ glasses case, crushproof	☐ plastic spade ☐ toilet paper
☐ 2 bandannas ☐ plastic bags, clear	
☐ 4 octopus straps	Food and Water
☐ notepad ☐ books ☐ pen or pencil	
☐ needles and thread	☐ 2 canteens or plastic water bottles
☐ flute, guitar, or baby grand piano ◇	☐ gorp or hi-energy snack food

Part C: Divide all these items, then give them to campers to carry

☐ two-man tents or larger tents	☐ food ☐ mixing bowls ☐ spatula
☐ tent poles, pegs, guy lines	☐ measuring spoons ☐ cooking pots
☐ backpacking water filter ◇	(use 1 two-quart pot for two persons)
☐ lantern (battery, kerosene, or oil)	☐ frying pan (use 1 large fp for 4
☐ fuel for lantern	persons) ☐ metal grill
☐ large first aid kit	☐ large spoon ☐ paper towels
☐ ax ◇ ☐ lg. spade ◇	☐ large knife in scabbard
☐ camping stoves ◇	☐ dishrags ☐ scrub brushes
☐ fuel for camping stoves	☐ dish soap (large bottle)
☐ plastic water jug, collapsible	☐ garbage bags (lg., biodegradable)

| DAY HIKES: EQUIPMENT LIST 3 ||
BRING:	NOTES:

Clothing (A)
 	
☐ backpack or knapsack (B)
☐ boots, walking shoes, or sneakers
☐ sweatshirt or sweater
☐ sandals (C)
☐ socks, 1 or 2 extra pairs
☐ brimmed cap ☐ 2 bandannas
☐ poncho or rain jacket ◇
☐ bathing suit ◇
☐ long pants (D) ◇
 	
Food and Water
 	
☐ 2 canteens or plastic water bottles
☐ A "no-cook, no-spoil" lunch
☐ gorp or hi-energy snack food
☐ spoon
☐ garbage bags, biodegradable
 	
Survival
 	
☐ swiss army knife or pocket knife
☐ first aid kit: ☐ adhesive tape
   ☐ gauze bandage ☐ bandages (12)
   ☐ soap ☐ petroleum jelly (for
     smothering ticks) ☐ tweezers
☐ first aid book (E)
☐ survival kit (F)
☐ ☐ maps and compass
☐ sunscreen lotion
 	
Personal
 	
☐ wwck: watch, wallet, cash, keys
☐ foot care kit: (☐ cornstarch or foot
powder ☐ moleskin pads ☐ bandages)
☐ glasses case, crushproof ◇
☐ toothpaste (G)
☐ important papers (H)
	A. This list includes everything except the clothes you will wear on the hike.
	B. A simple day pack, perfect for short hikes, can be made by sewing together old dungarees.
	C. Worth taking for 2 reasons: To air out your feet; and to walk in if your blisters get too bad to use your shoes.
	D. Needed if you're hiking in ticky woods or through leg-scratching vegetation.
	E. 3 good choices here: the American Red Cross First Aid manual; or a 1-page fact sheet (free from your local Red Cross) *First Aid At A Glance;* or the excellent booklet *Mountaineering Medicine,* available from Skagit Mountain Rescue Unit, P.O. Box 2, Mount Vernon, WA 98273.
	F. My survival kit contains: ☐ loose change (for emergency calls and "We'll be late for dinner" calls); ☐ emergency phone numbers; ☐ flashlight (waterproof & small); ☐ spare batteries; ☐ spare bulb; ☐ wood matches (waterproofed, in a waterproof container); ☐ pocket mirror for signaling; ☐ candle; ☐ fishhooks and nylon line; ☐ backpacking water filter; ☐ a twenty-dollar bill; ☐ 2 cans of sardines.
	G. Toothpaste: if necessary, brush your teeth with salt or baking soda
	H. Toilet Paper Tips: Remove the center cardboard and you can crush the roll flatter, to save space. Store tp in a plastic bag for waterproofing.

Appendix B:

THE ZORBA PRESS REGISTERED READER PROGRAM

It's FREE!!! And here are three more good reasons to join
the Zorba Press Registered Reader Program.

1. Free flyers. You automatically receive information about our new books and
   software, and other publications.

2. Free Technical Support. We will answer your camp counseling, child-maintenance,
   and other questions. If you would like answers to your questions, then
   You MUST enclose a self-addressed stamped envelope with adequate postage!!!

3. Permission to copy and use certain forms in this book, under the following terms:
   • You may not use the form(s) in any publication without permission from Zorba
     Press. You may not sell the form(s) or barter the form(s), or transfer the
     form(s) to another person.
   • You may not use the form(s) for teaching or training material, without
     permission from Zorba Press.
   • You may use the form(s) at one location only.
   • You may use the form(s) with your own group of campers only.

Forms in *Dynamite Counselors Don't Explode!* that Registered Readers may copy and
use are:

▤ Nature Trip Checklist (pp 82-3)   ▤ Activity Planning Worksheet (p 70)
▤ Equipment Lists (pp 112-114)   ▤ Get Found! Packet (p 85)
▤ Trip Emergency Info. Form (p 111) ▤ Camper Questionnaire (p 57)

How To Become A Zorba Press Registered Reader

Photocopy this form, then fill it out and return to:
Zorba Press, P.O. Box 666, Dayville, CT 06241, USA.

Name & Address:

Which Zorba Press Books/Products Do You Use?

How did you find out about Zorba Press books?
Optional: Comments or Biographical Information (use other side)

About The Author

Michael Pastore is the author of more than ten books, including *ZENLIGHTENMENT!* (1989), an anthology of illuminating quotations from the world's greatest literature; *LARK'S MAGIC* (March 1990) a comic novel for children ages 9 to 17; *DYNAMITE COUNSELORS DON'T EXPLODE!* (1993), a complete survival course for child-care workers and summer camp counselors; and *ZEN IN THE ART OF CHILD MAINTENANCE* (1993), a short comic novel. Mr. Pastore has taught writing seminars in Princeton, New Jersey; and has spent more than twenty summers working and playing with children of all ages and backgrounds. He has lectured on the subject of training adults to care for children at a number of camps, and at the 1993 American Camping Association National Conference. Currently, Mr. Pastore is the Camp Director for the Windham-Tolland 4-H Camp in Pomfret, Connecticut.

Great Books from ZORBA PRESS!

ZEN IN THE ART OF CHILD MAINTENANCE. By Michael Pastore.
Paperback 5.5" x 8"; 120 pages. ISBN: 0-927379-28-7. $ 14.95
ZEN IN THE ART OF CHILD MAINTENANCE is a short comic novel about the meeting between the extraordinarily beautiful Zenobia Goldbottom (Zen), and the world's most difficult nine-year-old: a wild and aggressive superbrat named Zerp. This entertaining story vividly and dramatically shows the reader how to respond creatively and lovingly to the misbehaving child. Also included in this volume are two short tales: *Fudge Unicorns, Chocolate Kangaroos*; and *Sunrises & Starry Nights*.

📖

DYNAMITE COUNSELORS DON'T EXPLODE! A Complete Survival Course for Child-Care Workers & Camp Counselors. By Michael Pastore.
Paperback 6" x 9"; 128 pages. ISBN: 0-927379-64-3. $ 14.95
Here in one lively volume is everything you need to know in order to effectively manage the modern child. The 20 chapters are packed with practical ideas, strategies, techniques, and games that you can use as soon as you open the book. Features chapters with 20 best outdoor games, 16 getting acquainted games, more than 50 Counseling Tips. Also includes an invaluable last chapter about how to find and get the best summer camp jobs. For new and experienced counselors alike. Foreword by Arthur Sharenow, CCD.

📖

ZENLIGHTENMENT! Insights into the art of living miraculously. Edited & prefaced by Michael Pastore. Paperback; 5" x 8"; 108 pages. ISBN: 0-927379-00-7. $ 15.00
ZENLIGHTENMENT! is a feast of wise sayings, electrifying passages, and remarkable remarks, each one pointing the way to happiness and inner peace. Thoreau, Emerson, Confucius, Shakespeare, Hesse, Lao Tzu, and Whitman are among the more than 100 Eastern and Western authors represented. Also included are 50 original, never-published-before gems of Eastern wisdom by Hokku Umeboshi & Ming Li.

📖

LARK'S MAGIC. By Michael Pastore. Paperback; 6" x 9"; 113 pages. Recommended for children ages 9 to 17. ISBN: 0-927379-36-8. $ 10.00
LARK'S MAGIC is the story of the wildest and cleverest kids to romp through the pages of a book since Tom Sawyer and Huck Finn. Readers will meet Brains, the ingenious boy-genius; Larquest Nova, who wears a mask to hide a shocking secret; and PDQ, the world's luckiest nincompoop. Together, the children unravel cryptic clues wrapped in rhyming riddles; discover the meaning of Lark's magic; and race against Time and sneaky villains in a daring attempt to rescue the Prince of Megoslavia.

Order Form for ZORBA PRESS Books

Qnty	ZP #	Title	Unit $	Total
	50	DYNAMITE COUNSELORS DON'T EXPLODE! A Complete Survival Course for Child-Care Workers & Camp Counselors	$ 14.95	
	36	ZENLIGHTENMENT! Insights Into the Art of Living Miraculously	$ 15.00	
	99	ZEN IN THE ART OF CHILD MAINTENANCE (short novel & stories)	$ 14.95	
	28	LARK'S MAGIC (children's novel)	$ 10.00	
			Subtotal	
			Plus Tax 6 % (CT res. only)	
			Shipping: for 1st book $3, for each additional book $ 1	
			Total	

PLEASE type or print. Mail the books to:

Name & Phone #

Address

Send check or
money order to:

Zorba Press, P.O. Box 666, Dayville, CT 06241 USA